T0384080

Cambridge Elements ≡

Elements in the Archaeology of Ancient Israel
edited by
Aaron A. Burke
University of California, Los Angeles
Jeremy D. Smoak
University of California, Los Angeles

EDOM IN JUDAH

Trade, Migration, and Kinship in the Late Iron Age Southern Levant

Andrew J. Danielson
University of British Columbia

CAMBRIDGE
UNIVERSITY PRESS

CAMBRIDGE
UNIVERSITY PRESS

Shaftesbury Road, Cambridge CB2 8EA, United Kingdom

One Liberty Plaza, 20th Floor, New York, NY 10006, USA

477 Williamstown Road, Port Melbourne, VIC 3207, Australia

314–321, 3rd Floor, Plot 3, Splendor Forum, Jasola District Centre,
New Delhi – 110025, India

103 Penang Road, #05–06/07, Visioncrest Commercial, Singapore 238467

Cambridge University Press is part of Cambridge University Press & Assessment,
a department of the University of Cambridge.

We share the University's mission to contribute to society through the pursuit of
education, learning and research at the highest international levels of excellence.

www.cambridge.org
Information on this title: www.cambridge.org/9781009517188

DOI: 10.1017/9781009424325

First published 2024

A catalogue record for this publication is available from the British Library.

ISBN 978-1-009-51718-8 Hardback
ISBN 978-1-009-42434-9 Paperback
ISSN 2754-3013 (online)
ISSN 2754-3005 (print)

Edom in Judah

Trade, Migration, and Kinship in the Late Iron Age Southern Levant

Elements in the Archaeology of Ancient Israel

DOI: 10.1017/9781009424325
First published online: November 2024

Andrew J. Danielson
University of British Columbia

Author for correspondence: Andrew J. Danielson, danielson.a.j@gmail.com

Abstract: During the late Iron Age (800–539 BCE) in the semi-arid southern Levant, small competing kingdoms navigated a tenuous position between their local populace and the external empires who dominated the region. For kingdoms such as Judah and Edom, this period was also one of opportunity due to their location at the intersection of lucrative trade networks connecting the Mediterranean and Arabian worlds. Such economic opportunity, together with subsistence practices rooted in mobility, resulted in a diverse and contested social landscape in the northeastern Negev borderland region between these two kingdoms. This Element explores the multifaceted interactions in this landscape. Insightful case studies highlight patterns of cross-cultural interaction and identity negotiation through the lenses of culinary practices, religion, language, and text. Ultimately, this analysis explores the lived realities of the region's inhabitants, migrants, and traders over multiple generations, emphasizing social diversity and entanglement as an integral feature of the region.

Keywords: Edom, Judah, Iron Age, archaeology, social entanglement

ISBNs: 9781009517188 (HB), 9781009424349 (PB), 9781009424325 (OC)
ISSNs: 2754-3013 (online), 2754-3005 (print)

Contents

1 Introduction

During the late Iron Age in the southern Levant (ca. 800–550 BCE), the semiarid region of the northeastern Negev formed the southern frontier of the kingdom of Judah. To the southeast in the highland region of present-day southern Jordan lay the kingdom of Edom. At first glance, the inhospitable arid zone between these kingdoms seems lifeless, and a barrier to any form of productive interaction (Figure 1). In reality, this frontier zone was crossed by a major trade route and generations of pastoralists, illustrating the constancy of connection and opportunities for engagement.

In the early archaeological excavations of the northeastern Negev of southern Judah (1960s through 1990s), substantial amounts of "foreign" material culture, primarily pottery, were excavated that were unlike local remains. The pottery, however, was markedly similar to that being excavated in Edom, and was quickly interpreted as "intrusive." The interpretations of the presence of this material culture were heavily shaped by literalistic readings of passages from the Hebrew Bible, which centered on a hostile invasion by Edomites (e.g., Aharoni 1981: 141–151; Beit-Arieh 1995a: 303–316, 1995c, 1996, 2007b: 331–334). Yet, subsequent analyses soon revealed that such interpretations were untenable, due to both the long-lasting nature of the so-called foreign material culture in the northeastern Negev, and the degree to which it was integrated – and even produced – at sites in the region (e.g., Whiting 2007; Thareani 2010; Tebes 2011b; Freud 2014; Singer-Avitz 2014).

Recent studies have built upon these analyses, further emphasizing connections across this arid borderland region, the lucrative economic opportunities afforded by it, and the resultant complexities of cross-cultural human interactions (Danielson 2020a, 2021, 2022, 2023). This Element summarizes and extends this body of work, aiming to further disentangle and problematize the notion of Judah and Edom as contrasting, homogenous social wholes, and emphasizing instead how mobility and interconnections were not only characteristic of the region, but an inherent part of its viability. In other words, cross-cultural interactions, migration, and the creation of different forms of kinship can be examined as integral to interactions between diverse groups in the region. Dynamic and networked understandings of intersecting and entangled identities allow us to reconceptualize the way(s) we view borderland regions in the southern Levant, and move toward more nuanced investigation of the complexities of ancient diversity and social entanglements.

This analysis begins with an examination of the geographic and sociopolitical context of the kingdoms of Judah and Edom in the late Iron Age (Section 2), followed by a discussion of the ways by which mobility and movement, particularly

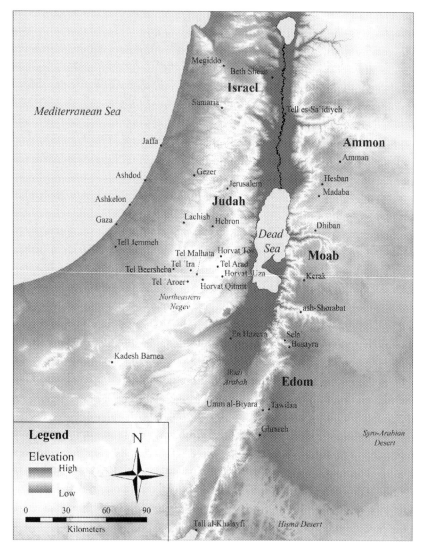

Figure 1 Map of the southern Levant in the late Iron Age

in relation to trade routes, were an integral part of the landscape (Section 3). Section 4 analyzes the archaeological record, using socially sensitive aspects of the material culture record as proxies for different aspects of identity, focusing on culinary traditions, religious practices, and dialect differences. Section 5 engages with the complex textual traditions of the Hebrew Bible that are associated with Judah and Edom, with a summary of the previous analyses drawn together in Section 6. Lastly, the epilogue describes the demise of this settlement system in the early sixth century BCE, and the roots of the textual traditions that sought to place blame for it on Edom.

2 Edom and Judah in Context

The late Iron Age (ca. 800–550 BCE) in the southern Levant was marked by a series of small competing kingdoms negotiating their place in a challenging landscape and beneath increasing external imperial pressures. These kingdoms coalesced around cities, kin groups, and regions, forging new relationships and social structures. They were, however, neither predetermined fixtures in the landscape, nor homogenous in their makeup. Rather, they were created things, and structured through the vision of elite individuals or coalitions who possessed the ability to create and enforce sociopolitical unity (Routledge 2004; Porter 2022).

These kingdoms, often centered around discrete regions, can be seen as "invented and reinvented" at different times in their history, to follow Benjamin Porter's description (2022: 619). Using the kingdom of Moab to illustrate, Bruce Routledge has demonstrated how a close reading of the iconic Mesha Inscription (ca. 850 BCE) reveals a programmatic effort to integrate different kin structures and regions into a coherent political entity, labeling it with an existing regional term – Moab (2004: 133–153). In this understanding, there is then the continual need on the part of ruling persons and groups to (re)create and reinforce relationships to maintain sociopolitical cohesion and internal hierarchies, often by re-envisioning kinship structures (Sergi 2019), through propagandizing visual displays (Hogue 2022), and through the careful negotiation of force and consent (Routledge 2004: 213–217).

As such, these political experiments did not function as monolithic sociopolitical entities exerting homogenous control over a territory (Agnew 1994).[1] Rather, emphasizing the inherent negotiations that form the center of political experiments and the human engagements that constitute and reify them, it can be more productive to envision elite activity and the formation of political control as operating through a network. In this model, human – especially elite – action can be seen as gravitating toward specific strategic nodes in the landscape (rich in resources, access to water, junctures of major routes, etc.), and the corridors of access between them (Smith 2005). In this way, political action or shared cultural practices, for example, need not necessarily be sought in contiguous locations, particularly when considering the (semi)arid nature of the far southern Levant (Osborne 2013; Danielson 2020a: 47–51, 2022; Hogue 2022). With these considerations in mind, we can turn to Edom and the northeastern Negev.

By all accounts, the sedentary late Iron Age highland kingdom of Edom located in southwestern Jordan arrived onto the southern Levantine political stage quite late. It is only in the late eighth century BCE that clear markings of

---

[1] This is the trap of "methodological nationalism," which assumes that the "nation-state" serves as an elemental political building block (Wimmer and Schiller 2002), as is too often assumed for the Iron Age Levant (Osborne 2020: 1–4).

the establishment of elite authority can be identified. These markings center on the construction of elite administrative and ideological structures at Busayra, namely the construction of a palace (Area C) and an adjacent temple (Area A) atop the acropolis of the major fortified center (Bienkowski 2002a; Porter 2004). The building of these structures highlighted Busayra as the focal point of political and religious authority, with the intentional placement of these buildings adjacent to one another serving to mark the position of the ruling elite as sanctioned by their local, dynastic god – Qos (*qws*; קוס; Danielson 2020b: 119–127).[2]

Concurrent with the establishment of Busayra is a significant increase in the number of sedentary settlements in the highlands of southern Jordan. It is difficult to assign firm dates to this rapidly increasing process, but based on the pottery remains, it would seem that they were roughly contemporaneous to, or perhaps slightly preceded the establishment of Busayra, increasing in number throughout the eighth century BCE (Smith et al. 2014: 284–287; Bienkowski 2022). These settlements, however, are unique in relation to Busayra. For example, the majority of them are quite small (< 1 ha), and are unfortified, appearing to be small farmsteads or hamlets. There do not appear to be any sites in highland Edom at which clear evidence for secondary elite administration can be identified.

Combined with this settlement portrait is the phenomenon of "mountaintop" sites (e.g., Baʿja III, Jabal al-Khubtha, Qurayyat al-Mansur, Jabal al-Qseir, as-Sadeh, as-Selaʿ, Shag Rish, Umm al-Biyara). These naturally fortified and difficult-to-access sites appear to evidence regional strongholds operated by disparate kin groups that were not always aligned with the Busayran elite, or that at least presented the potential for a strong counterpoint to centralized rule (Lindner and Knauf 1997; Bienkowski 2011). As such, Edom, despite displaying widespread cultural similarity on the basis of material culture remains, does not appear to have been highly integrated or centralized. Rather, political power in Edom appears to be present in more of a "malleable territoriality" or

---

[2] Recent work in the Wadi Arabah has argued for an earlier phase to the kingdom of Edom, dating from the Iron Age I through the early Iron Age II (twelfth–ninth centuries BCE; Levy et al. 2014; Ben-Yosef et al. 2019). This purported early phase of Edom is argued to have consisted of a mobile, non-sedentary sociopolitical entity based in the lowland regions, and focused at the copper mining and production centers at Faynan and Timna (Ben-Yosef 2019, 2021). Despite aspects of continuity identified in the ceramic record (Smith 2009), the two described "phases" of Edom are remarkably different. As Piotr Bienkowski (2022) has recently outlined, it is not possible to identify similar settlement patterns, any related forms of increasing complexity, or any technological continuity in copper production. Further, the lack of direct chronological continuity, as marked by a gap of 50 to 100 years, indicates that these two entities were organized according to different patterns, thus challenging that these two Edoms represent the same sociopolitical entity.

"network" model (Smith 2005; Osborne 2013; Crowell 2021: 375), wherein Busayra's authority was inconsistent throughout the region with direct control only well evident in its immediate hinterland (Smith et al. 2014: 287–290; Bienkowski 2022: 12–13), and at sites along corridors of strategic significance (e.g., Danielson 2023: 155–159; Danielson and Fessler 2023).

By contrast, the monarchic tradition of the kingdom of Judah centered in Jerusalem predated that of Busayra. Despite the debate over its early history (van Bekkum 2023), Jerusalem served as a center for elite authority, with the palatial center drawing legitimacy from its temple. Jerusalem's control over the surrounding regions fluctuated over time, but broadly encompassed the Shephelah, Judean Highlands, and northeastern Negev. Similar to the previous description for Edom, however, it is necessary to emphasize that this political authority was the result of constant social negotiations, evolving over centuries. Similarly, while the Shephelah, Judean Highlands, and northeastern Negev were the broad regions under the influence of Jerusalem, by no means was this political power fully bounded and homogenous, much less so the social identities of its inhabitants. Of these regions that were at times influenced or dominated by the kings of Judah, it is in the northeastern Negev that the majority of this analysis focuses.

The northeastern Negev is located at the southern edge of Judah, alternatively called the Beersheba-Arad Valley (or Nahal Beersheba) after the two major sites that lay at either end of this east-west running valley system. The northeastern Negev was home to several waves of thriving settlement systems during the Iron Age, owing in part to its function as an access corridor connecting the Mediterranean to regions to the south and east. In particular, during the ninth and eighth centuries BCE, this settlement system consisted of Tel Beersheba, Tel ʿIra, Tel Malhata, and Tel ʿAroer as the main fortified towns, with the fort of Tel Arad to the northeast monitoring the access road through the highlands to Hebron and Jerusalem. A series of destructions at these sites at the close of the eighth century BCE – attributed to the campaigns of Sennacherib and the Assyrian Empire – created a brief period of disruption that was followed by rapid rebuilding and expansion in the seventh century BCE (Table 1).

With the exception of Tel Beersheba, which was not rebuilt, each of the aforementioned sites was reoccupied, with the administrative role held by Tel Beersheba and Tel Arad in the previous century maintained at Tel Arad (Garfinkel and Mendel-Geberovich 2020), with Tel ʿIra (Ramat Negeb?) likely taking on aspects of the former role of Tel Beersheba. Moreover, the seventh century BCE saw expansion, particularly in the addition of the fort at Horvat ʿUza and its watchtower Horvat Radum at the eastern access point to the valley, the fort at Horvat Tov on the road north to Jerusalem, a religious site on the hill at Horvat

Table 1 Comparative stratigraphy of the northeastern Negev
and surrounding region

Comparative Stratigraphy of the Northeastern Negev and Surrounding Region

	Iron I	Iron IIA	Iron IIB	Iron IIC	Babylonian Period	Persian Period
	1,000 BCE	900 BCE	800 BCE	700 BCE	600 BCE	500 BCE · 400 BCE
Tel 'Ira		VIII	VII · VI———		V	IV
Tel Beer-sheba		VII VI V IV III	II I–‹			
Tel Malhata		V	IVB IVA· IIIB IIIA—‹			
Tel 'Aroer			IV III IIa IIb—‹		Ia	
Tel Arad		XII	XI X–VIII VII VI———			
Horvat 'Uza			?——III——‹			
Horvat Radum			?——I——‹			
Tel Masos			?–Area G—‹			
Horvat Qitmit			?—I—‹			
Kadesh Barnea	IV		III II——‹		I	
'En Hazeva	VI	V	IV————‹			
Kuntillet 'Ajrud		I ———				

Qitmit, and a yet poorly understood occupation at Tel Masos. As will be discussed presently, one of the primary features of this settlement system was its east–west orientation along the floor of the Nahal Beersheba. In particular, this valley served as an efficient westward route from the Wadi Arabah and southern Jordan toward the Coastal Plain, intersecting with additional roads north to Jerusalem and southwest through the desert to Egypt. As such, this region was the center of long-standing patterns of mobility and east–west movement, with numerous instantiations of settlement and activity floruits over the millennia (Finkelstein 1995; Koch and Sapir-Hen 2018; Danielson 2023).

2.1 Geography and Environment

The region of Edom is commonly identified with the highland region of southwestern Jordan, south of the Wadi al-Hasa (biblical Zered) and north of Ras en-Naqb that marks the southern delineation of the highlands. To the east lies the arid Syro-Arabian Desert, and to the south, the Hisma Desert, which extends through the Hejaz region of northwest Arabia. This highland region of Edom is framed along its western extent by a mountainous range, with the Wadi Arabah beyond. The term Edom (אדם) itself, meaning "red," appears to be derived from the reddish color of the Nubian Sandstone massifs running north-south along the eastern side of the Wadi Arabah (Bartlett 1992: 287; Danielson 2020a: 74–84). The term "Seir" (שעיר) also often appears in relation to Edom, at times appearing to designate a mountainous subset of the greater region of Edom (Genesis 14:6, 32:3, 36:8), and at other times functioning as a near synonym (Genesis 32:3; 36:8; Knauf 1992a; Edelman 1995: 7–11).

While these topographical features in effect served to delineate and constrain human movements, they by no means function as a strict "border" for the region as in fact there is significant evidence of material culture and elite Edomite activity beyond this region, most notably at Tall al-Khalayfi (formerly Tell el-Kheleifeh) at the southern end of the Wadi Arabah along the Red Sea, and in the northeastern Negev. In fact, while the label Edom can be understood as first a regional term, later co-opted as a political and gentilic designation, its geographic contours likely shifted at different times and included regions from the Negev to the west (Edelman 1995: 7–11; Ben-Yosef 2021: 161–166).

The core of the region of Edom on the highland plateau was located in a Mediterranean vegetation zone, characterized by a Mediterranean maquis forest featuring species of oak, olive, pine, and terebinth. Dwarf shrubs and other herbaceous flora are also common, with ideal rainfall patterns reaching 200 to 400 mm per year (Figure 2;[3] Cordova 2007: 90–94; Langgut et al. 2014, 2015). While the Mediterranean vegetation zone at the heart of Edom was well suited for dry farming and horticulture, it was geographically limited. Surrounding it was the more arid Irano-Turanian zone, a drier landscape suited to more limited rainfed agriculture, but ideal for range pastoralism (Figure 3). Beyond, the remainder of southern Jordan was situated in the Saharo-Arabian desert zone, in which only a limited range-based pastoralism – dependent on a specialist knowledge of water sources – was possible (Cordova 2007: 95–104; Ababsa 2013: 64–90; Kagan et al. 2015).

The kingdom of Judah to the northwest broadly comprised the regions of the Shephelah, Judean Highlands, and northern Negev. To the east and southeast of the political and ideological center at Jerusalem, the arid Judean Desert presented a difficult and hostile landscape, contrasted with the more advantageous environmental situation of the Shephelah to its west and southwest. This more

---

[3] Note that these rainfall amounts are averages, and that rainfall on yearly or decadal intervals can fluctuate significantly. For communities living on the 200 mm per annum rainfall threshold – viewed as the minimum required for successful dry farming – fluctuations could have a significant impact on successful harvests, necessitating a varied subsistence regime.

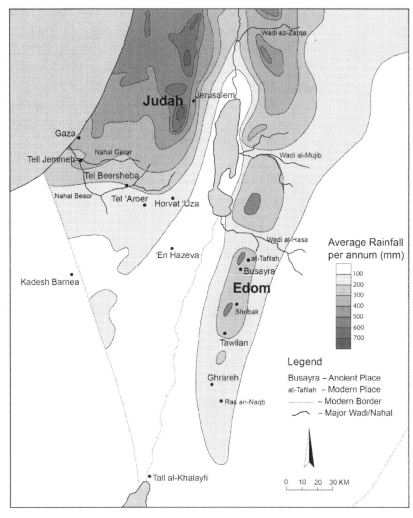

Figure 2 Average rainfall patterns of Edom and the Negev (map by author; data after Israel 1985: Map 12; Ababsa 2013: Fig. I.12)

fertile region of Judah consistently received approximately 300–600 mm of rainfall per annum (Langgut et al. 2015), with its resultant Mediterranean vegetation zone well suited for agriculture and horticulture, particularly viticulture and oleiculture (Finkelstein et al. 2022).

The northeastern Negev of southern Judah, however, was more marginal than central Judah, receiving only about 100 to 300 mm of rainfall per year. Similar to large parts of Edom, vegetation in this nearly treeless Irano-Turanian zone was restricted primarily to species of grasses and shrubs (Cordova 2007: 95–104; Langgut et al. 2015: 219). For subsistence purposes, it was suited to less reliable

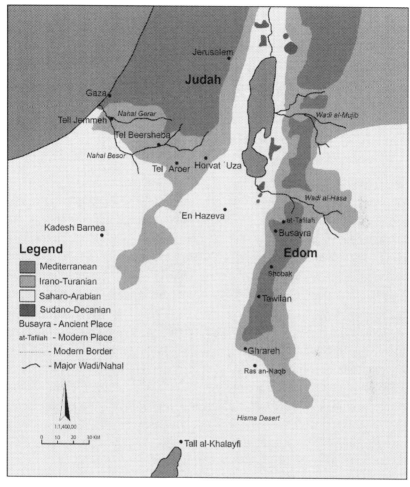

Figure 3 Vegetation zones of the southern Levant (map by author, after Langgut et al. 2015: Fig. 1)

rainfed farming, but better suited to pastoralism. In the Negev to the south, and the Wadi Arabah that lay between the northeastern Negev and Edom, the landscape shifted again into desert (Saharo-Arabian Zone), suitable for limited range pastoralism, though reliant on a specialist knowledge of the region (Cordova 2007: 104–121).

Perhaps most significant to the northeastern Negev, was the east-west oriented Beersheba-Arad Valley that crossed it, with its perennial springs, settlements, and forts, establishing it as an ideal route by which to cross from the Wadi Arabah to the Coastal Plain. At its eastern end, the valley was entered from the northern Arabah likely via the Nahal Heimar, a route guarded by the fort at Horvat ʿUza and its subsidiary towers (Cohen-Sasson et al. 2021), with a secondary route entering the Beersheba-Arad Valley from the south in the environs of Tel ʿAroer (Ben-Yosef et al. 2014: 546, Fig. 6.39). At its western end, the Beersheba-Arad Valley linked with the Nahal Gerar to the northwest and the Nahal Besor to the southwest, both of which intersected on the Coastal Plain at the site of Tel Jemmeh, a supremely important junction in the southern Levant.

2.2 Negotiating Autonomy in an Imperial World

The independent nature of southern Levantine kingdoms, particularly Judah and Edom, was never a given. Their small size and marginality often resulted in influence from neighboring kingdoms and empires, if not outright control. During the late eighth century BCE, the geopolitical situation in the southern Levant was fraught. The expanding Assyrian Empire had threatened the southern Levant for more than a century, and now under the vigorous leadership of Tiglath-Pileser III began to seize more direct control. In particular, the conquest of Damascus in 732 BCE ushered in an era of southern Levantine subservience to Assyria, with nearly every king subsequently recorded as providing tribute and entering into "client" status (Westbrook 2005). The Assyrian sources identify a named king of Judah – Ahaz – presenting tribute to Tiglath-Pileser III at this time (Koch 2022: 694), and name Qausmalak of Edom as similarly entering into client status through tribute payments (Crowell 2021: 111–114). From this period onward, the southern Levant, in particular Judah and Edom, became formally entangled in the Assyrian Empire, with Assyrian expectations of tribute and access to strategic sites.

The close of the eighth century BCE was punctuated by a significant disruption, at least in relation to Judah. Following the shocking and untimely death of Sargon II in Anatolia, Hezekiah of Judah sought to break free from Assyria, encouraged and aided by Egypt. Despite the "victory" claimed by Judah as the city of Jerusalem was not destroyed, Sennacherib's 701 BCE suppression of the rebellion is widely attested archaeologically in destruction levels at numerous sites throughout Judah, marking a clear shift in the settlement system of the region (Faust 2008; Koch and Sapir-Hen 2018: 439). Archaeologically, these destructions are convenient as they permit a diachronic comparison between the late eighth and seventh century BCE phases of the settlements (Danielson 2020a: 133–140). Edom does not exhibit the same pattern of destruction as it does not appear to have participated in the rebellion. Despite the rebellion, throughout the seventh century BCE and until the gradual dissipation of Assyrian influence ca. 630 BCE, Judah and Edom continued to function as client kingdoms of the Assyrian Empire.

In fact, in the case of Edom, the arrival of Assyrian influence may have served as a catalyst for the establishment of a ruling elite at Busayra. As previously discussed, it was not until the late eighth century BCE that the trappings of elite authority could be detected in the sedentary settlements of the highlands, especially visible in the construction of the palatial and temple complexes on the acropolis of Busayra (Porter 2004: 384–387). These structures have long been noted for their Assyrian influence, most notable in their use of podia (*tamlû*), and the architectural forms of the temple and palace (Reich 1992: 219–220; Bienkowski 2002a: 94–95, 199–200, 478–482). Their late eighth century BCE date is thus quite striking when considered in tandem with Assyrian records of tribute, and with the named Qausmalak drawing Edom into client status with Assyria.

Assyrian influences in construction, however, need not imply formal Assyrian presence, as there remains little compelling evidence for Assyrian occupation or even the presence of Assyrian officials (Bennett 1982: 187; Crowell 2021: 356–357). Considering the unique ways that the "Assyrian" features are not exact replicas of Assyrian elements and the ways by which southern Levantine traditions were interwoven with them, more compelling explanations highlight local architects influenced by Assyrian architects or visits to Assyrian courts, with the Assyrian features lending prestige to local contexts of authority (Reich 1992: 214–215; Porter 2004: 385–386; Brown 2018b: 66–70; Danielson and Fessler 2023). The contemporaneity of the creation of political authority at Busayra with the advent of client status to Assyria is not meant to imply that the creation of sedentary sociopolitical complexity necessitated Assyrian influence. Rather, at this time, a confluence of circumstances created an opportune moment in which ambitious elites in the region could formalize and expand their own power. Notably, elite symbols of dominance, readily visible from the expanding, alluring, and seemingly inevitable Assyrian Empire, presented an accessible and impactful repertoire by which to communicate such authority.

Similarly, this influence and prestige can be detected in certain pottery forms, forms that were inspired in part by Assyria but thoroughly indigenized in local tradition. In the southern Levant, and in Edom in particular, the presence of "Assyrian-style" pottery has long been noted (Glueck 1967; Mazar 1985), often overstating their "Assyrian" elements and implying the local varieties to be derivative, with influence and prestige unidirectional. More recent studies have since emphasized the social and regional contingencies of the specific forms found in the corpus from Edom (Thareani 2010; Tebes 2011b), and the ways by which the unique painted decorations on many of the vessels evoke a more North Arabian tradition (Tebes 2013, 2015) that could be linked to certain contexts and modes of consumption (Danielson 2020a: 244–251, 2022: 128–133).

Indeed, when considering the "Assyrian-style" forms from the southern Levant more generally, Alice Hunt (2015) has stressed the ways that local agency resulted in specific modes of use for certain forms that are not a reflection of their use in the Assyrian heartland. In particular, Hunt's analysis of the corpus from nearby Tell Jemmeh demonstrated significant differences in form, surface treatments, and usage patterns from Assyria, concluding that they served different social and semiotic functions that reflected the local population's perception of Assyria, and their relation to its empire (Hunt 2015: 146–181). In this way, as we see in the pottery from Edom, the selective adoption of certain forms of consumption vessels that are integrated in a broader corpus, and are further decorated in motifs and patterns that are specific to the region, demonstrate a local adaptation of prestige objects that evoke a particular relationship with Assyria while serving the needs of the local population.

Returning then to the larger narrative, the formalization of sociopolitical complexity in a sedentary form centered at Busayra appears to have coincided with the arrival of Assyrian dominance in the southern Levant, and as will be discussed presently, with factors including the flourishing of the South Arabian trade. Assyrian interest in the Levant, beyond ideological conquest and the proximity of Egypt, lay in its ability to extract wealth and resources as is evident in the tribute lists associated with conquest and client subservience (Dalley 2017; Koch 2022: 701–702). As such, one of the goals of Assyria in the southern Levant appears to have been the creation of a "frictionless" corridor for Assyrian military personnel, as well as the transfer of goods back to Assyria (Fessler 2016; Danielson and Fessler 2023). In this model, the southern Coastal Plain and the Assyrian investment at Tell Jemmeh were quite significant as they stationed Assyrian authority at a position where they could benefit from the confluence of Arabian, Levantine, and Mediterranean trade networks, at the border with Egypt (Koch 2018: 371–375). Targeted control over this region, with a particular emphasis on sites including Tell Jemmeh (Ben-Shlomo 2014), allowed Assyria to maximize influence and wealth with the least amount of investment (Thareani 2016: 94–95).

Provided tributes were paid, Assyria presented something of a laissez-faire approach to local polities, positioning agents of their empire in strategic locations, and relying on local elite collaborators to manage the diverse polities and populations throughout the region (Faust 2021: 131–132, 209–210). This situation is particularly apparent in late Iron Age Transjordan – especially Edom – where Assyria only ruled indirectly through local proxies who navigated a tenuous position between their local populations and external imperial rulers, ensuring loyalty and tribute payments to Assyria (Porter 2004; Yamada 2005: 79–80; Faust 2018: 30–36). In such a context, Craig Tyson's emphasis on the idea of the peripheral elite as imperial collaborators is particularly cogent

(2018). Using the kingdom of Ammon as an example, Tyson has explored this idea to emphasize the agency of the local elite, analyzing the ways by which they maximized their own positions within society while serving as intermediaries with the Assyrian Empire (Thareani 2017: 417–418; Tyson 2018). This heuristic can similarly well explain the diverse forms of Assyrian "influence" seen throughout Edom, while positioning them within a framework that highlights the role of the local elite in navigating transregional politics, utilizing their own local, specialist knowledge to maximize their position.

3 Mobility and Local Foreigners in the Northeastern Negev

Despite its seemingly inherent marginality, the Negev was by nature highly conducive to mobility and movement that worked to embed diversity within its social fabric. For example, the integral role of pastoralism in the region and the necessity of herd pasturage and management would promote a degree of mobility at a foundational level (Koch and Sapir-Hen 2018: 433–437). More significant though, is the geography and topography of the region that connected the Mediterranean ports of the Coastal Plain for trade purposes with inland regions, namely southern Jordan and Arabia (Singer-Avitz 1999; Koch and Sapir-Hen 2018; Danielson 2022: 117–120, 2023; Finkelstein et al. 2022: 271–272).

In fact, the unique affordances of the east-west oriented Beersheba-Arad Valley in the northeastern Negev that allowed for efficient east-west access was a feature in earlier centuries and millennia (Finkelstein 1995; Yahalom-Mack 2017). In particular, in the Iron I–IIA, during which the mobile non-sedentary polity often described as "Early Edom" operated in the Arabah (Ben-Yosef 2019; Ben-Yosef et al. 2019),[4] copper export was facilitated via the same route (Yahalom-Mack 2017; Klassen and Danielson 2023), as well as through the Negev Highlands (Ben-Dor Evian 2017). During this period, links with Arabia are similarly evident in the numerous exemplars of Qurayyah Painted Ware, originating in the Hejaz region of North Arabia, whose distribution can be traced along this route (Tebes 2007b; Intilia 2013).

During the late Iron Age, the expanding settlement system of the northeastern Negev was linked to a branch of a major trade route extending to South Arabia (Figure 4; Finkelstein 1992; Singer-Avitz 1999; Tebes 2006a, 2007a; Danielson 2023). The rapid increase in importance of this Negev branch of the route appears to be connected to the fall of Damascus in 732 BCE and the arrival of Assyrian hegemony, resulting in the opening of new routes (Byrne 2003). The settlement expansion in the northeastern Negev and rise in Arabian trade also coincides with the establishment of a sedentary sociopolitical hierarchy in

---

[4] See n.2.

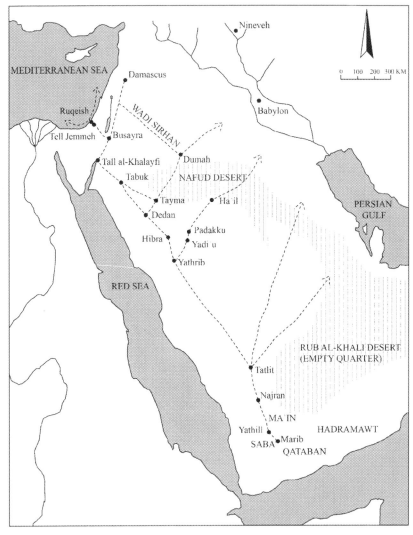

Figure 4 Map of Arabian oases and trade routes (map by author, adapted after Macdonald 1997: Fig. 1)

highland Edom, suggesting that their fortunes were to a degree intertwined (Danielson 2023: 142–151, 155–163). While the lucrative nature of trade with South Arabia is better known in its later Nabatean and Roman instantiations (Plin. *HN* 12.30–32, 41; Strab. 16.4.22–24), the origins of this trade with the Levant and the establishment of the networks that facilitated it were rooted in the Iron Age II. The most prized components of this trade included aromatics, specifically frankincense (*Boswellia*), which was native to South Arabia where the unique ecology allowed these trees to grow. Definitive evidence of frankincense as one component of the broader Arabian trade has been identified on residues from a late eighth century BCE altar from the temple at Tel Arad, providing a *terminus ante quem* for the origins of the aromatics trade in relation to the southern Levant (Arie et al. 2020).

Direct archaeological evidence for this trade is difficult to identify due to the mutability of many of its components and the transitory nature of the trade. Yet, numerous proxy identifiers allow for the contours of this trade to be elucidated. First, while very few of the so-called "incense altars" common to this region have had residue analyses conducted on them, and while there is evidence for other varieties of locally sourced (lower-prestige) incense,[5] the positive identification of frankincense on the Tel Arad altar suggests that these altars may serve as a partial indicator for the realia of this trade. Similarly, the necessity of the camel (*Camelus dromedaries*) as a requirement for the trans-Arabian trade,[6] and the excavation of camel remains at points in this network with evidence for their use as pack animals, provides further evidence (Wapnish 1981; Hakker-Orion 2007: 289; Fedele 2014, 2017). Lastly, the distribution of inscriptions bearing Arabian scripts, names, or linguistic elements scattered throughout the southern Levant formally signals the identity of many of the traders and other connections with Arabia (Danielson 2023: 149).

The geographic distribution of these proxy remains (Figure 5) visually demonstrates the presence of trade with Arabia as well as outlining a major route of its movement through the northeastern Negev (Danielson 2023: 147–150). More specifically, however, an inscription discovered in South Arabia records the itinerary of one such caravan endeavor. Among a lengthier list of exploits, the inscription describes a caravan from South Arabia that traveled through Dedan and the "towns of Judah" (*'hgr yhd*) to reach Gaza, prior to sailing to Kition on Cyprus (Bron and Lemaire 2009). While there remains some ambiguity regarding the date of the inscription,[7] the route described appears to cross directly through the northeastern Negev, and on the basis of the settlement patterns in the region, would certainly fit

---

[5] The locally sourced *Commiphora gileadensis*, otherwise known as "Balm of Gilead," was of a lesser quality than its South Arabian counterparts and appears to have been in less demand (Jeremiah 8:22; 46:11; Ben-Yehoshua et al. 2012: 1–2).

[6] The unique ability of the dromedary to survive in harsh, arid regions while simultaneously serving as a pack animal signals it as a necessity for sustained and robust trans-Arabian trade to be conducted. Consensus holds that the domestication of the dromedary in Arabia is only well established in the early first millennium BCE (Magee 2015), and similarly, the domesticated dromedary as a pack animal only appears in the southern Levant in the early first millennium BCE, with widespread evidence for its use only increasing in the ninth and eighth centuries BCE (Sapir-Hen and Ben-Yosef 2013).

[7] While the inscription is unprovenanced, it appears to originate from Nashq in the kingdom of Saba', present-day al-Bayda, Yemen. While Bron and Lemaire suggest an early sixth century BCE date (2009), other proposals, based on aspects of paleography, lean toward a date up to the early fourth century BCE (Multhoff 2019).

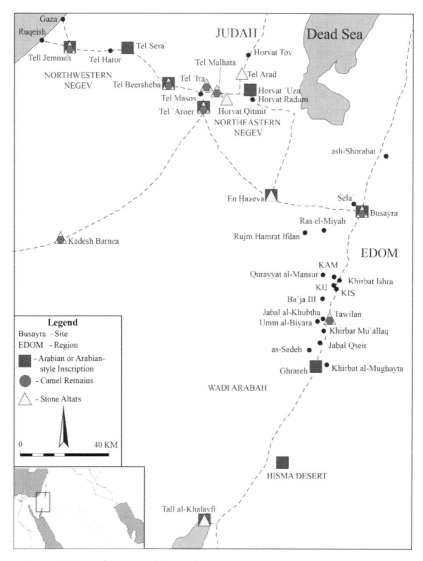

Figure 5 Map of proxy evidence for Arabian trade in the southern Levant, eighth–sixth centuries BCE

in a seventh or early sixth century BCE context. Taking these factors into account, and including the frequent references to Arab communities in contemporary Assyrian sources, a robust picture of the Arabian trade and its movement through the southern Levant can take shape (Eph'al 1982: 74–169; Retsö 2003: 119–234).

While the aromatics are heralded as the most lucrative of the trade goods moving northward from South Arabia, it bears emphasis that these were but one traded item among many moving through the broader networks of caravan trade. References in biblical texts identify a diversity of products moving northward from distinct locales in Arabia. For example, from the Hejaz region of northwest Arabia, saddlecloths are listed as a prized product of Dedan, and lambs, rams, and goats from Qedar (Ezekiel 27:20–21). From southwestern Arabia, Sheba (Saba᾽) and Raamah are associated with trade in aromatics, precious stones, and gold (Ezekiel 27:22). Similarly, increasing Assyrian contact and campaigns against the Arabs, from the reign of Tiglath-Pileser III through the reign of Esarhaddon, cumulatively highlight aromatics, camels, people, and precious stones as some of the major tribute and traded items of Arabia, with the latter likely serving as an efficient mode of exchange (Retsö 2003: 148–159; Danielson 2023: 143–145).

Regarding material goods traded south from the Levant and Syria, records of raids on caravans returning to South Arabia record the capture of purple cloth, wool, precious stones, and iron (Cavigneaux and Ismail 1990). Similarly, in the biblical text's description of the trade partners of Tyre, Judah and Israel are described as trading in "wheat ... millet, honey, oil, and balm," and Edom as trading in "turquoise, purple, [colorful weaving],[8] fine linen, coral, and rubies" (Ezekiel 27:16–17).[9] Likewise, as noted in relation to records of Assyrian wars against the Arabs, the forcible movement and displacement of humans, as prisoners of war and enslaved people, was also a factor along these networks (Eph῾al 1982: 21–59). Trade in captured and enslaved people is also intimated in the biblical text of Amos, which contains invectives against Gaza and Tyre for "delivering entire communities over to Edom" (Amos 1:6, 9). Notably, the route connecting Gaza and Edom alluded to in Amos is the same route under discussion in this work.

In all, the previous discussion highlights trade as a major economic aspect of the southern Levant, and Edom and the northeastern Negev more specifically. Further, a major result of this trade would have been its contribution to the east-west movement through the region, bringing people to and taking people from it, and presenting additional economic opportunities associated with the caravans (e.g., provisioning, protecting, etc.). Of similar significance, the functionality and profitability of the established network would have also drawn the attention of opportunistic persons and polities seeking to exploit it. Far from representing isolated regions, numerous modes of connectivity and movement

---

[8] Many translations favor "embroidered work" for "רקמה" though a translation in the sense of variegated colors in woven material is equally justifiable (Koehler and Baumgartner 2001: 1291).

[9] Aram (ארם) is preserved within the Masoretic Text, though a reading of Edom (אדם) is preserved in multiple manuscripts and is to be preferred (Lindsay 1976: 30; Sedman 2002: 408–409). Due to the graphic similarity of *rêš* and *dālet*, these two place names are at times mislabeled for one another in the biblical text (Lemaire 1988). For example, see also the duplication of Dedan (דדן) in Ezekiel 27:15 and 20, where the former ought to be Rhodes (רדן; *rōdān*).

may be identified between southern Jordan the northeastern Negev. These connections resulted in multifaceted modes of cross-cultural interactions that would create and reinforce identities through experiences with others.

4 Identity Negotiation and Social Entanglements

Tracking cross-cultural interactions through archaeological and textual material culture is a challenging process. First, queries need to focus on what is meant by identity and its varied terminological manifestations. Much of the following section will explore differences at a broader, social or cultural scale. In doing so, it is necessary to grapple with terms such as "nationality" or "ethnicity" and the ways these are often (mis)used in such analyses. Further, considerations need also to be given to questions of intersectionality and how status, gender, and age factor into the lived experiences of ancient individuals and discussions of identity (e.g., Diaz-Andreu et al. 2005).

It is especially important that the labels of "Edom/Edomite" and "Judah/Judahite," not immediately be assumed to correlate with a homogenous ethnicity (or nationality) that can be directly equated with excavated material culture. While these terms were certainly used in the textual and inscriptional record of the ancient world, their use is most commonly as an etic referent, used to refer to specific regions, and the political entities, communities, or individuals found therein.[10] Thus, the title of this work that highlights "Edom" and "Judah" as two seemingly monolithic and homogenous entities, is something of a misnomer. These terms reflect broad labels most often applied by external entities for expedient identification, or by the ruling elite who pursued a broader argument for social cohesion over the diverse groups they sought to rule (Routledge 2004: 133–153; Danielson 2022: 120–121; Porter 2022: 622–627).

Further, assumptions of "national" identities as identifiable in the archaeological record betray the nature of the data available, applying modernist ideas to a context that was structured and functioned quite differently (Routledge 2003). Notably, ideas of nationality in the present are inherently reliant and interwoven with concepts of delineated borders, territorial forms of bordered sovereignty, and with the implied rights and responsibilities associated with citizenship that were not features of our ancient context. Likewise, significant scholarship has highlighted the inherent challenge (and often inappropriate) modes by which "ethnicity" has been sought in the archaeological record, undercut most substantially by the fact that "ethnicity" as a category of identity,

---

[10] For example, see 1 Samuel 21:7 in the reference to "Doeg the Edomite," or 2 Kings 20:21 with the reference to Joram who "attacked the Edomites." In these instances, we see "Edomite" used as an external, etic label for an individual or groups associated with the region/kingdom of Edom. It is not used as a self-referent.

ought not to be assumed as the primary structuring principle of the archaeological record (Jones 1997; Lucy 2005; Twiss 2019: 130–138; Damm 2022: 92–93). Rather, what we can seek to highlight are patterns in the archaeological record that demonstrate shared practice. When such shared practices can be identified in relation to broader social patterns and can further be compared or contrasted to different practices, we can ultimately reconstruct diverse aspects of ancient identities.

In identifying these shared practices in the archaeological record, we must resist the urge to immediately associate these patterns with labels such as "Edomite" or "Judahite," as doing so applies an external homogenizing label to individuals and communities for which these terms likely held little meaning. In contrast, if we were to focus on emic statements of self-identification, these labels would center on parentage or place. For example, from the northeastern Negev, excavated ostraca preserve the records of individuals who chose to describe themselves through kin relations (e.g., Gedalyahu son of 'Uriyahu) and/or in relation to a discrete place (e.g., 'Imadyahu son of Zakkur, from Moladah; Beit-Arieh 2007a: 139, 153). Such emic referents serve to re-center the individual in their immediate context of meaning, highlighting in this instance their relation to nearby locality and/or parentage or kin group. Such labels of identity, however, are quite limited in scope and are difficult to associate with archaeological material culture.

Amidst these challenges, we do see shared practices that extend over areas that are much broader than a town or kin group. The following section will examine aspects of the material culture record that extend over broader areas, indeed at times overlapping with the regions and political groups that bear the labels of "Edom" or "Judah." First, however, these patterns in material culture will need to be examined in relation to the *practices* associated with them. Thus, for example, analyses of cooking pots highlight patterns in culinary practices, and dialect differences highlight patterns in regional and social speech communities. These cannot be a priori assumed as all coherently related to a specific ethnic or national group, or fully equating with other material culture proxies for different aspects of identity. Lastly, it is necessary to consider the role that elite power holds in such discussions of broader social cohesion and the very real ways that elite political or religious agents work to foster and shape ideas of collective similarity and cohesion. With these ideas and caveats in mind, we can now turn to an examination of the archaeological record to delineate different aspects of identity, cross-cultural interaction, and social entanglements. These small snapshots into ancient lifeways and interactions will center on culinary practices, religious practices, language and dialect, and their respective roles in creating and negotiating identities.

4.1 Foodways: Maintaining and Trespassing Tradition

Food stands at the center of social interactions. To begin a broader discussion on culinary practices in the northeastern Negev, a cultural memory from the biblical text provides a unique window into some of the theoretical concepts associated with foodways studies. Discussed in further detail in Section 5.1, the Jacob and Esau narratives from the latter portion of Genesis are notable for their etymological and etiological understandings of the origins of Judah/Israel and Edom as from these legendary patriarchs (Genesis 25, 27, 32–33). The setting of the narrative is in this region, and its redaction is contemporary to this late Iron Age context and the centuries following (Finkelstein and Römer 2014).

The Jacob and Esau narratives center on the competitive, fraternal relations between the twin figures of Jacob and Esau, with a portion of the text devoted to Esau somewhat unwittingly losing his birthright to the younger Jacob. Amidst this contention, two meals take place. The first consists of hunted game prepared in a "savory" (מטעם) way that was presented with bread and wine to the patriarch of the family, Isaac, in a setting of social significance, indicating a degree of prestige placed on the (hunted) meat (Genesis 27:17). The second meal consists of a red lentil stew (נזיד עדשים; Peters 2016: 117–119), prepared by Jacob, but desired in a significant enough way by Esau to "trade" his birthright for it (Genesis 25:29–34). The text plays on the meaning of "red," seeking to etymologically and etiologically associate the meal with Esau and Edom. From these meals consumed by the legendary patriarchs of these regions, we see first a prestige placed on the consumption of meat, and second, that an iconic food dish literally stood at the center of the interactions between Jacob and Esau, who stand in the narrative as metaphors for Judah/Israel and Edom.

This identification of food as at the center of interactions between the brothers, but at the same time more abstractly, the metaphorical social groups they represent, highlights a key feature of foodways study. That is, the importance placed on food beyond its role for subsistence. Food stands at the center of diverse and scaled social engagements, from routine family meals to celebrations of the creation of social bonds (e.g., marriage), and to large commemorations of religious events. Due to repetitive consumption primarily in group settings, food can become imbued with emotion, standing at the forefront of ideas of heritage and holding a powerful semiotic role in its social milieu (Appadurai 1981; Brulotte and Di Giovine 2014).

Understanding food then as socially sensitive as well as culturally conservative, allows it to serve as a readily identifiable marker of identity, creating distinction between groups, with those who eat similar food viewed positively, and those with unrecognizable foods viewed with distrust or even disgust

(Twiss 2012, 2019). Numerous studies have engaged with the ways that cuisine can be used to express association with a certain social identity, particularly among immigrant communities or in culture contact situations (Brighton 2015; Franklin 2015; Danielson 2021; Damm 2022). In such contexts, numerous examples can be seen where traditional foodways are maintained over successive generations, even when separated from places of origin (Ben-Shlomo et al. 2008; Fantalkin 2015). Likewise, as food procurement and preparation are often a gendered activity, they can allow for a more nuanced examination of aspects of the household economy (Meyers 1988: 146–147, 2007; Gero and Conkey 1991).

The Jacob and Esau narrative also highlights another key feature of foodways that can be traced archaeologically – cooking pots. In the text, these material objects are highlighted by the act of "boiling" (נזיד), or cooking different ingredients to produce a distinctive and desirable meal (Shafer-Elliott 2013: 148–156; Peters 2016: 117–119). In the archaeological record of the southern Levant, cooking pots are ubiquitous. Due to daily thermal stresses, cooking pots tend not to survive for long periods of time. Their short-lived nature accentuates their ubiquity, and allows for the tracking of morphological variations. More importantly, in the absence of residue analyses, the fabrics and forms of vessels can provide insight into different cuisines, recipes, and ingredients. For example, different sizes of vessel openings permit differently sized ingredients and different levels of liquid evaporation, with certain fabrics ideal for higher or lower temperatures. Cumulatively, these factors result in diverse textures and tastes of the food prepared in certain types of pots (Rice 1987: 239–240; Tebes 2011b: 87–88; Magness 2014: 50–51; Danielson 2020a: 241–244). As coarse wares used in non-performative settings, cooking pots are likewise seldom the objects of trade between different cultural groups. Combined with their socially sensitive nature, and the fact that in pottery production the rigid nature of complex motor habits required to produce certain forms are only attained through years of immersive apprenticeship, cooking pots tend to serve as strong indicators of the presence of their bearers and/or producers (Dietler and Herbich 1998; Gosselain 1998; Nelson 2015). Lastly, the identification of standardized locales of production for cooking pots in the late Iron Age emphasizes the understanding of their regionalized use (Ben-Shlomo et al. 2023).

The culinary landscape of the southern Levant was dominated by the so-called Levantine triad: bread (wheat, barley), wine (grapes), and oil (olives; Macdonald 2008: 19–24; Pace 2014: 187–189). Evidence for the centrality of these foods in the diet of the northeastern Negev can be found in the Arad Ostraca where various combinations of flour (קמח) or bread (לחם), oil (שמן), and wine (יין) are listed as the rations provided for persons associated with the

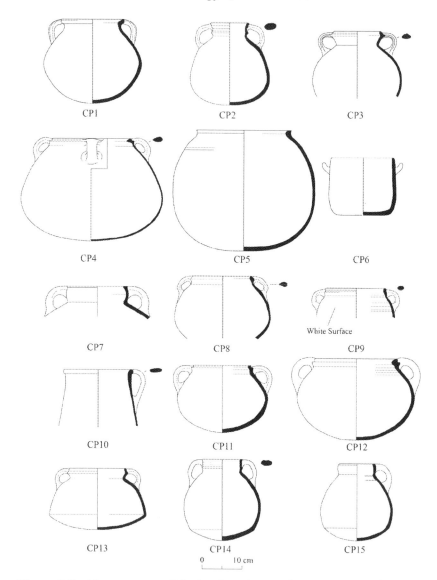

Figure 6 Cooking pot types of the late Iron Age northeastern Negev (figure by
the author; vessel forms adapted from Singer-Avitz 2002: Fig. 14:6, 15:9; Freud
2007: Fig. 3.41:9, 2015: Fig. 4.132:2)

military administration in the region during the late seventh and early sixth
centuries BCE (Aharoni 1981: 12–38; Pace 2014: 188). While forming staple
pillars of the diet, however, these were supplemented by a variety of vegetables,
particularly legumes (e.g., lentils, peas, vetch), and fruits (e.g., fig, date, pomegranate, apple), dairy as a secondary product from sheep and goats, meats from

domesticated animals (especially sheep and goat), a variety of hunted species (e.g., gazelle, deer, ibex, hare, boar, etc.), and imported fish (Macdonald 2008; Danielson 2020a: 191–193, 221–224).

Various combinations of these foods, based on preference and availability, would result in dishes that were both flavorful and familiar. Certain ingredients, such as meat, would have been restricted to more festive occasions, elite contexts, or ritual activity (King and Stager 2001: 68; Magness 2014: 35). In an average house, up to three meals would be eaten daily, with the main meal in the evening consisting of a type of vegetable (and meat?) stew, flavored with herbs and sopped up with bread (Genesis 25:29–34; Ruth 2:14; King and Stager 2001: 67–68). Hunted game or imported fish could supplement the diet for those with the means by which to acquire them (Genesis 25, 27; Pace 2014: 193–194). Consumed foods, however, would also be constrained by geography, social status, and gender, with those at lower social levels lacking access to greater nutritional diversity, and likely women consuming less prestige food, like meat, than their husbands and sons (Macdonald 2008: 91–93). Nonetheless, the continued preparation and consumption of such foods over time would result in a network of entangled recipes, cuisines, and practices perpetuated by different social groups in different regions.

4.1.1 Food Production and Cooking Vessels

While a single type of cooking pot was not necessarily restricted to a single cuisine, and apart from residue analyses determining ingredients, different cooking pot types do signal variant practices, and through differences in size and form, variant culinary traditions. Geographic patterns in the distribution of specific cooking pot types can then reveal insights into the culinary traditions that were preferred in certain regions or at certain sites. During the late Iron Age, no less than fifteen distinct cooking pot forms can be identified in the northeastern Negev and southern Jordan (Figure 6). Each form presents its own history and distribution resulting in unique social narratives. For example, Type CP10 is represented by only a single exemplar at Tel Malhata, but possesses a form and fabric that originated in the Aegean (Freud 2015: 201; Danielson 2020a: 164, 482). Alternatively, Type CP13 was dominant at the site of Tel Beersheba in the eighth century BCE, but appears to not have been well-used beyond this site (Danielson 2020a: 165, 485). As detailed analyses of these cooking pot forms have been presented elsewhere (Danielson 2020a: 147–251, 420–488, 2021, 2022: 122–128), the following discussion will track only some of the most dominant forms from the late eighth through the early sixth century BCE, presented in Table 2.

Table 2 Descriptions of major cooking pot (CP) types of the late Iron Age northeastern Negev

Type	Description	Regional patterns and date range[11]
CP1	Neckless CP with an everted rim and two handles; often called a "Judahite" CP.	Common in Judah, Iron IIC.
CP2	Ridged-neck CP with two handles; often called a "Judahite" CP.	Common in Judah, Iron IIC.
CP3	Stepped-rim CP with an out-flaring neck with two handles; often called a "Coastal" CP.	Common in the Beersheba–Arad Valley, but better-known in the southern Coastal Plain, Iron IIC.
CP4	Neckless or short-neck CP with a ridged rim, and two to four handles; often called an "Edomite" CP.	Dominant in southern Jordan, but also well attested in the northeastern Negev; predominantly Iron IIC, although it also appears in late Iron IIB.
CP5	Simple rim or holemouth CP with incipient or no handles. It is often handmade and presents numerous localized subvariants. It is often called an "early" Edomite CP, and is similarly at times called "Negevite," though differentiated from CP6 in this typology by its lack of a flat base.	Attested throughout southern Jordan and the northeastern Negev; dates predominantly to the Iron IIB, but is also present in Iron IIC.
CP6	Handmade CP with a flat base; also called a "Negevite" CP or krater.	Common in Iron IIB and IIC, as well as in earlier centuries; attested in southern Jordan, at Tall al-Khalayfi and at Kadesh Barnea, although not attested in the northeastern Negev.

[11] For a detailed list of attested exemplars and comparative typologies, see Danielson (2020a: 158–166, 2021: 91).

To demonstrate distinct culinary practices at different sites, we can turn to two forts from the northeastern Negev: Horvat Tov and Horvat ʻUza. Both of these sites date to the seventh and early sixth centuries BCE, and on the basis of geography, material remains, and the rich inscriptional corpus from Horvat ʻUza, are securely identified as operated by the Judahite military administration (Beit-Arieh 2007b; Itkin 2020). Beginning with Horvat Tov, a near-uniform picture of culinary practices emerges. The fort is dominated by cooking pots of the CP1 and CP2 variety (Figure 7). These forms present both an open (CP1) and closed (CP2) cooking pot type that is dominant in the region at this time, demonstrating why the label "Judahite" has often been applied to them. The shared geography of these open and closed forms

Horvat Tov

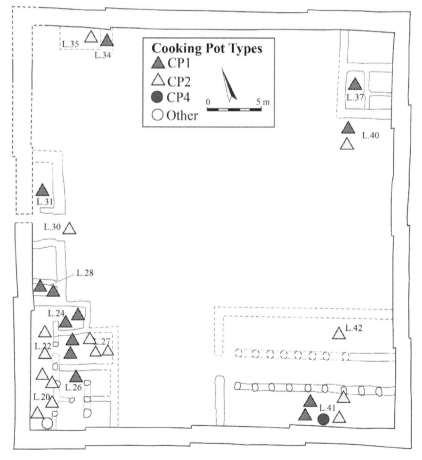

Figure 7 Cooking pot types at Horvat Tov

suggests that they reflect different aspects of a related cuisine. The open, wider-rimmed CP1 pots could have been used to produce drier stews with the option of larger ingredients (bones, meats?), whereas the closed CP2 form was better suited toward moisture retention, but with its restricted opening limiting the size of ingredients. The near ubiquity of these forms at Horvat Tov is broken by one vessel dissimilar to those found in the northeastern Negev, and by a single exemplar of Type CP4. Excavated in the pillared structure in the southern corner of the site and in the same context as two exemplars of both CP1 and CP2, the Type CP4 cooking pot is notable not only in its isolation at the site, but in its own context of excavation.

Turning to the site of Horvat ʿUza, a rather divergent portrait emerges. Whereas, similar to Horvat Tov, types CP1 and CP2 are the most common, types CP3 and CP4 are also present, accounting for 20 percent and 15 percent of the overall assemblage respectively (Figure 8). The picture of culinary practices here is clearly more complex. The form CP3 with its out-flaring neck represents a type that is well attested in the Coastal Plain to the west. Similarly,

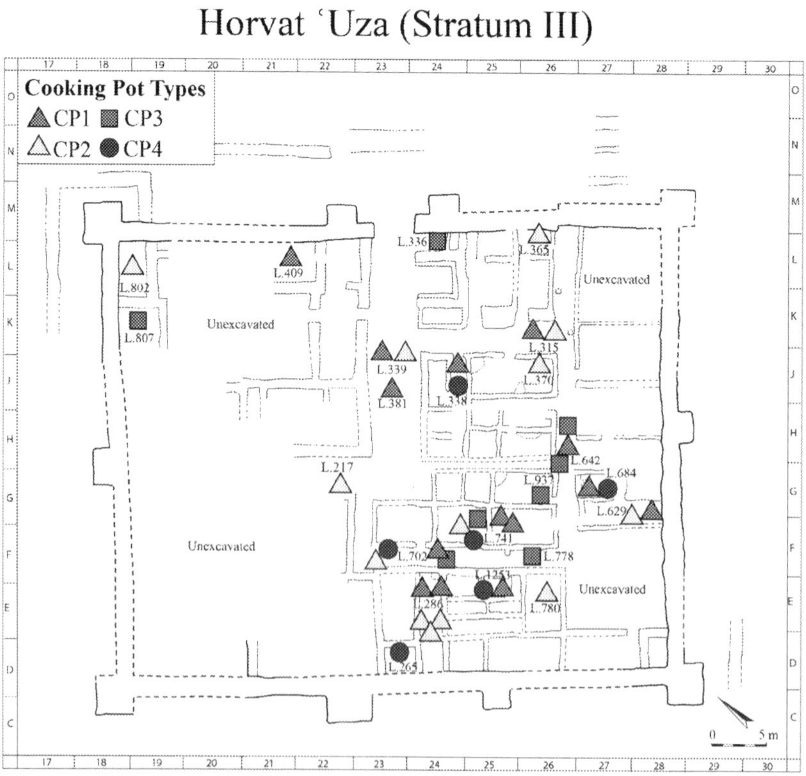

Horvat ʿUza (Stratum III)

Figure 8 Cooking pot types at Horvat ʿUza

while only present in a single exemplar at Horvat Tov, CP4 is common at Horvat ʿUza. Notably, however, both types CP3 and CP4 are not restricted to certain areas in or outside the fort, but are found scattered throughout. In fact, in contexts such as L.741 in the south-central area of the site, we find that all four types of cooking pots were excavated in the same domestic structure. If their location of deposition matches their use context, then diverse foods were prepared in the same space. Despite their contemporaneity and operation by the same political entity, Horvat Tov and Horvat ʿUza present starkly different portraits of culinary practice.

Here, geographic location and our understanding of routes through the northeastern Negev is of importance. Notably, while Horvat ʿUza was located on the major east-west route running from southern Jordan to the Mediterranean, Horvat Tov was located a distance northward, on a north-south branch off this highway.[12] Horvat ʿUza's position along a route connecting eastern and western regions – that each presented its own specific traditions – appears to have afforded it greater culinary diversity. In contrast, Horvat Tov's location along a less-traversed route, and more deeply embedded in Judah, may have resulted in a more restricted culinary repertoire. Indeed, if one takes a broader perspective of the geographic distributions of cooking pots, an interesting pattern emerges.

When the relative quantities of excavated cooking pots are mapped spatially, a strong correlation between CP1 and CP2 emerges (Figure 9). Both forms are present in relatively similar quantities, and are prominent in the northeastern Negev and at Kadesh Barnea, but have not been excavated to the east. A single exemplar of CP1 has been published from Tall al-Khalayfi, where it was clearly a rare form. Type CP3, discussed previously in relation to Horvat ʿUza, is fairly well attested in the northeastern Negev, though at a lesser scale than CP1 and CP2 (Figure 10). In contrast, its distribution is accentuated to the west, where it is prominent at Tel Jemmeh, and while not depicted in Figure 10, is dominant in the Coastal Plain to the north, comprising for example, more than 90 percent of the cooking pot assemblage at seventh century BCE Ashkelon (Stager et al. 2008: 86–87). This type is also well represented at Kadesh Barnea, intimating a high degree of connection between this site and the Coastal Plain.

In contrast to the previously discussed forms that are prominent in the northeastern Negev, CP4 is overwhelmingly the most dominant type in southern Jordan, present at every site for which there is available data: from ash-Shorabat in the north to Tall al-Khalayfi in the south (Figure 10). Alongside the presence

---

[12] Note that Tel Arad, near to Horvat Tov, bears a very similar cooking pot assemblage to it (Danielson 2021: 97–99).

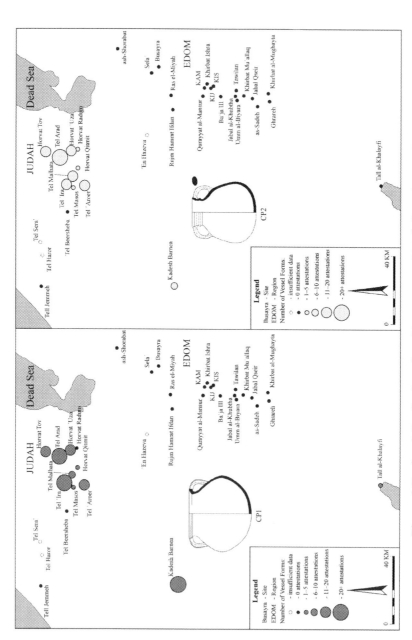

Figure 9 Regional distribution of cooking pot type CP1 (left) and CP2 (right)

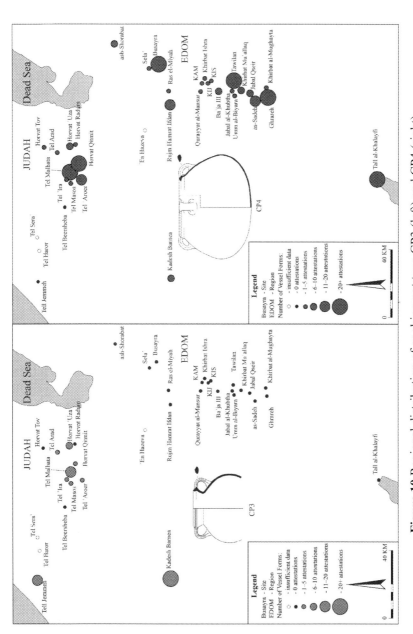

Figure 10 Regional distribution of cooking pot type CP3 (left) and CP4 (right)

of CP4 in southern Jordan are other well-known types (e.g., CP5, CP6, CP7, and CP8), though all are infrequent forms in comparison (Danielson 2020a: 158–163, 172–193, 475–480). Yet, CP4 is also attested at nearly every site in the northeastern Negev, though most prominently at the religious site of Horvat Qitmit, and the fortified towns of Tel Malhata and Tel ʿAroer. A similar, though less accentuated pattern can be identified for CP5, which similarly is known throughout southern Jordan and also the northeastern Negev at Tel Malhata and Tel ʿAroer, where it derives primarily from eighth century BCE contexts (Figure 11; Danielson 2020a: 435, 444–446). Its similarity in form and chrono-logical relation to CP4 has led Liora Freud to suggest that the latter form developed from, and replaced, the former (2015: 196). To highlight a final cooking pot type, CP6 is common in southern Jordan, particularly at Tawilan, Ghrareh, and Tall al-Khalayfi, and is also known at Kadesh Barnea, though not in the northeastern Negev (Figure 11). The long-lived nature of this form and its correlation with the more arid locales suggests its use among communities active in the desert regions (Haiman and Goren 1992; Martin and Finkelstein 2013).

While the distributions of these forms suggest restricted regional use for certain cooking pot types (e.g., CP2), contrasted with wider use by other forms (e.g., CP4), it is necessary to further examine the contexts of production. As pottery production areas or kilns are lacking from the excavations in the northeastern Negev, we can turn to petrographic analysis of the clay fabrics to determine likely clay sources, and Instrumental Neutron Activation Analysis (INAA) to determine chemical similarity between vessels. Of the cooking pots excavated in the Negev, petrographic analysis of types CP1 and CP2 has identified predominantly terra rossa soils, likely originating in the Shephelah or central Judean Highlands to the north (Iserlis and Thareani 2011: 181; Freud 2014: 302). Comparisons to similar vessels throughout Judah have led David Ben-Shlomo et al. to suggest specialized production centers for these and other cooking pots, perhaps in the vicinity of Jerusalem (Ben-Shlomo et al. 2023; Bouzaglou and Ben-Shlomo 2023). As such, these cooking pots stand in contrast to many of the other non-cooking pot vessels from the northeastern Negev that were instead made from the local loess (Iserlis and Thareani 2011: 179–183; Ben-Shlomo et al. 2023: 100).

The petrographic analysis of Type CP3 cooking pots identifies many as belonging to the Coastal Hamra soil group, indicating an origin on the Coastal Plain to the west, while others petrographically belong to the sandstone group of the Hazeva formation, suggesting they were produced in the environs of the northeastern Negev or northern Arabah Valley (Freud 2014: 286–287, 292). Petrographic analysis of Type CP4 vessels excavated at Tel Malhata, Horvat

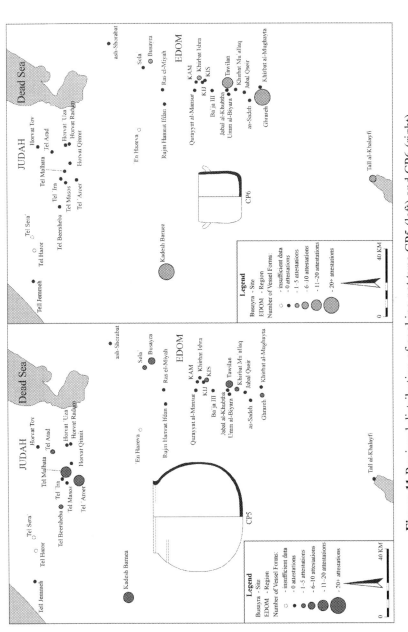

Figure 11 Regional distribution of cooking pot type CP5 (left) and CP6 (right)

'Uza, and Horvat Qitmit have determined that they similarly belong to the sandstone Hazeva formation, produced in the environs of the eastern Negev or northern Arabah (Freud 2014: 285–286, 289–291). Notably, several Type CP4 vessels from Tel 'Aroer have been associated with Lower Cretaceous shales that may have originated in the highland region of southern Jordan (Iserlis and Thareani 2011: 180–182).[13] From southern Jordan, only INAA results are available (from Busayra, Tawilan, Umm al-Biyara, and Ghrareh), and only in limited numbers for Type CP4 cooking pots. Nonetheless, the INAA results have shown that the vessels from southern Jordan are chemically dissimilar from those in the northeastern Negev, indicating different locales of production (Gunneweg and Mommsen 1990, 1995: 281, 285–286; Gunneweg et al. 1991; Gunneweg and Balla 2002).

While less petrography has been done on Type CP5 vessels, examples from Tel 'Aroer and Tel Malhata have similarly identified them as deriving from the sandstone Hazeva formation, suggesting again, production in the vicinity of the northeastern Negev or northern Arabah Valley (Iserlis and Thareani 2011: 181; Freud 2014: 302). INAA analysis of a single Type CP6 "Negevite" cooking pot amidst a greater sample from Kadesh Barnea, has tentatively suggested an origin in Edom, with the greater "Negevite" corpus showing numerous examples deriving from both the Negev and southern Jordan (Gunneweg et al. 1991). Petrographic analyses of this type of vessel from earlier centuries (e.g., Martin and Finkelstein 2013) have established diverse contexts of production and use, highlighting their association with mobility.

The emergent portrait of cooking pot distributions and contexts of production is striking. Both CP1 and CP2 vessels appear closely related to one another, and signify the culinary traditions most deeply rooted in the late Iron Age landscape of the northeastern Negev and regions to the north, where they were produced. The diverse assemblage at Horvat 'Uza appears to exemplify the east-west connections of this site, with the CP3 forms linking with traditions to the west and the CP4 forms to common traditions in southern Jordan. Yet, notably, many of the CP4 forms from the northeastern Negev – including those from Horvat 'Uza – were produced locally (Freud 2014). Thus, CP4, and its likely forebear CP5, represent traditions local to the northeastern Negev for at least a century and a half, highlighting a complex series of overlapping and intersecting culinary traditions. And yet, a diversity of practices was not attested at every site.

Just as Horvat Tov and Horvat 'Uza presented different culinary traditions, we can turn to two additional sites to compare: Tel 'Ira and Tel Malhata. These latter

---

[13] Since the regions around Makhtesh Gadol, Makhtesh Qatan and Makhtesh Ramon also present Lower Cretaceous shales, the origins of these clays are not necessarily in southern Jordan (Sneh et al. 1998; Freud 2014: 297–300).

sites present multiple strata from the eighth through sixth century BCE, allowing for diachronic analyses of their culinary traditions. To begin, Tel ʿIra presents two major relevant strata: Stratum VII dated to the late eighth century BCE, and Stratum VI dated to the seventh through early sixth centuries BCE. The cooking pot forms are presented in Figure 12, where the center "mixed" stratum identifies the cooking pots in contexts that could not confidently be assigned to either Stratum VII or VI. Both of these strata, however, contain a fairly restricted number of cooking pot forms, with the earlier level presenting an overwhelming number of types CP12 and CP14, and Stratum VI presenting an overwhelming abundance of types CP1 and CP2, with the mixed strata maintaining the same general pattern, albeit mixed. While not discussed previously, the prominent Stratum VII types CP12 and CP14, represent the major open and closed cooking pot forms of the eighth century BCE northeastern Negev (Danielson 2020a: 165–166, 484, 486), effectively mirroring the subsequent role of CP1 and CP2. Accordingly, due to the inherent "local" nature of these earlier forms, Tel ʿIra appears to exhibit considerable culinary stability over successive centuries, evolving to a degree, but remaining remarkably consistent. The assemblage is not entirely homogenous, however, as three exemplars of Type CP3 and three additional exemplars of CP4 are attested, but these latter forms comprise a minority.

Tel Malhata, located less than 4 km to the southeast, presents a stark contrast. Here, three main strata are available for analysis: Stratum IV of the eighth century BCE, Stratum IIIB, and Stratum IIIA dated to the seventh through early sixth centuries BCE. While types CP12 and CP14 are similarly well represented together with an additional, local, open form CP11, other forms are common (Figure 13). A significant number of Type CP5 are attested, together with a significant number of Type CP4, signifying both its longevity in the northeastern Negev and its popularity. In the early seventh century BCE (Stratum IIIB), there is continuity in the use of local cooking pot types CP11, CP12, and CP14, as well as the introduction of the prominent seventh century BCE CP1 and CP2 forms (Figure 14). Notably, however, during this phase Type CP4 became the most prominent, accounting for 33 percent of the overall assemblage (Danielson 2021: 101–102). This portrait of CP4 prominence increases in the subsequent Stratum IIIA until the destruction of the site in the early sixth century BCE. In this final phase, Type CP4 accounts for 42 percent of the overall assemblage, with the newly introduced Type CP3 similarly prominent (24 percent). Types CP1 and CP2 are also attested, though as part of a distinct minority. The diversity of cooking pot types is also identifiable in the same activity (or discard) areas at Tel Malhata exemplifying that these traditions existed adjacent and with one another, rather than in isolation (Danielson 2020a: 206–211, 444–456, 2021: 101–103).

Tel ʻIra (Stratum VII)

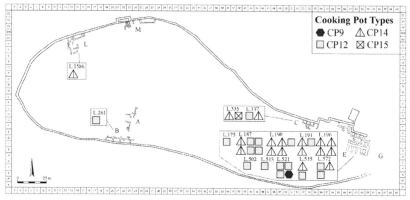

Tel ʻIra (strata VII-VI, mixed)

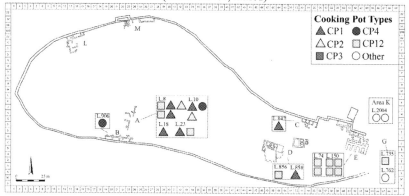

Tel ʻIra (Stratum VI)

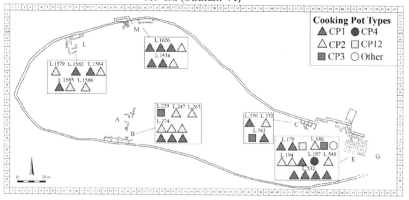

Figure 12 Cooking pot types at Tel ʻIra

Despite their proximity to one another, Tel Malhata presents a vastly different culinary story than Tel ʻIra. The contrast seen between Horvat Tov and Horvat ʻUza, presented in a contemporaneous moment, can be teased out diachronically

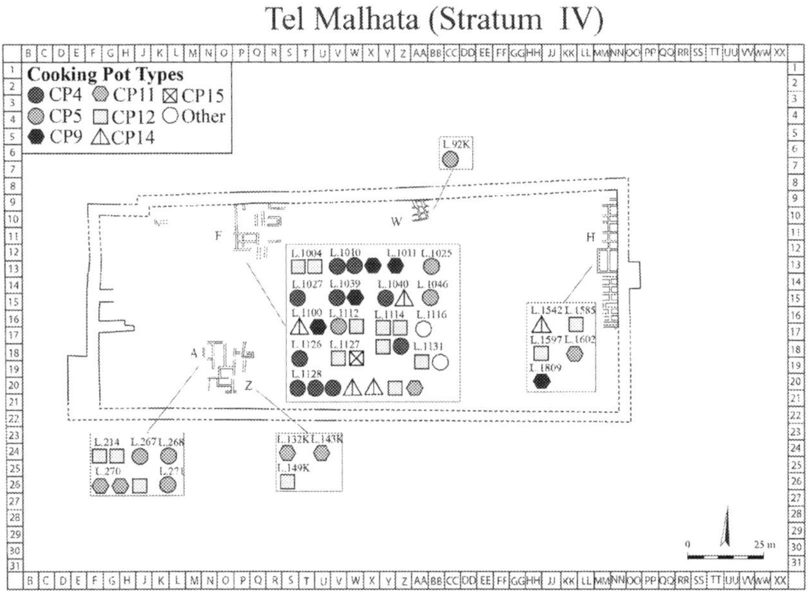

Tel Malhata (Stratum IV)

Figure 13 Cooking pot types at Tel Malhata, Stratum IV

at Tel ʿIra and Tel Malhata, where the former's relatively stable homogeneity can be contrasted with the increasingly diverse set of culinary traditions at the latter. These differences likely indicate variant social preferences and activities occurring at diverse sites. In particular, we can also determine that geographic positioning as well as site functionality played a role in the patterning of culinary practices. For example, Horvat Tov's restricted assemblage can be compared to Tel Arad, another Judahite fort located on the north-south road. With these forts, we might also consider Tel ʿIra, whose similarly restricted assemblage of cooking pots is identifiable over successive strata. This large fortified site was located at a higher elevation along the northern side of the valley, and if its identification as Ramat Negeb is correct, may have served an important military/administrative role for the region during the seventh century BCE, perhaps assuming the role held by Tel Beersheba in the preceding century (Aharoni 1981: 46–49; Thareani 2011: 5). While also a military fort, Horvat ʿUza presents the same major types but with increasing diversity. Here, its location along the major east-west route is likely a central factor driving the diversity that approaches the degrees of complexity seen at Tel Malhata and Tel ʿAroer. These latter, culinarily diverse sites, represent significant nodal points along the major east-west trade route through the region.

At an immediate practical scale, these divergent cooking pot forms represent connections between their users and the locations where the vessels were made.

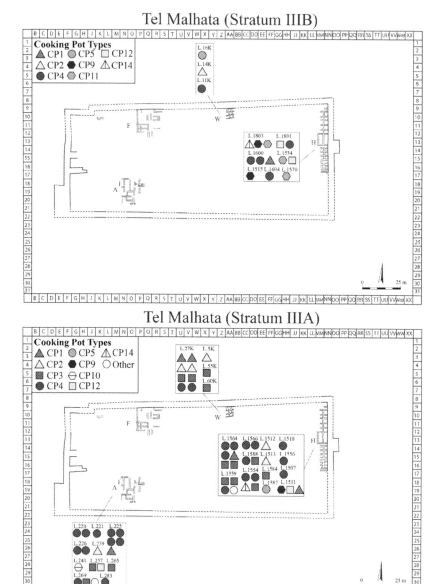

Figure 14 Cooking pot types at Tel Malhata, Stratum III

The aforementioned petrographic analyses of the cooking pots are now beginning to identify regional production centers, likely due in part to the higher technical skill necessary to produce durable cooking wares, and the surrounding regions that imported them (Ben-Shlomo et al. 2023). This situation especially applies to types CP1 and CP2, whose terra rossa soil type and similarity to other forms suggest a locale of origin likely in the Jerusalem area (Ben-Shlomo et al. 2023: 99–101; Bouzaglou and Ben-Shlomo 2023). As such, connection, exchange, and movement between these locales were responsible for the presence of these forms, exemplifying that this directionality in culinary (and social) orientation was particularly prominent at sites such as Tel Arad, Horvat Tov, and Tel ʿIra. Here, their association with the military administration of Jerusalem, and their nearness to the north-south road appears to have affected their culinary traditions.

In contrast, vessels like CP4, produced in the northeastern Negev or northern Arabah, represent an entirely different set of connections and exchange as well as production techniques (Bouzaglou and Ben-Shlomo 2023). Despite their formal similarity to corresponding vessels in southern Jordan, CP4 vessels from the northeastern Negev appear to have been largely, though not exclusively, locally produced (Freud 2014). Nonetheless, their shared forms suggest a broader shared culinary tradition (Danielson 2021). Yet, this tradition did not suddenly "appear" in the northeastern Negev, but was established already as early as the late eighth century BCE as seen at Tel Malhata (see Figure 13; Singer-Avitz 2014). Further, if Liora Freud's hypothesis holds, that Type CP5 forms a precursor that evolves into Type CP4 (Freud 2015: 196), then our perspective on the rootedness of this tradition in the northeastern Negev becomes even more accentuated.

And yet, as certain imported forms suggest, and as the rapid increase in popularity of CP4 and CP3 in the seventh century BCE indicates, these traditions were supplemented through natural population growth as well as the introduction of new persons to the region (Danielson 2021). In such contexts of immigration, the maintenance of familiar culinary traditions is not only unsurprising, but to be expected. Beyond the maintenance of traditional culinary practices, the cooking pot forms from southern Jordan are found amidst a broader web of diverse practices and preferences that intersected with local traditions in a complex and entangled network that did not always fully overlap or integrate (Danielson 2022). Just as Horvat Tov and Tel Arad maintained a preference for CP1 and CP2 forms, the inverse can be seen at the religious site of Horvat Qitmit. Here, 80 percent of the overall forms were of Type CP4, which together with iconography and inscriptions, identify the site as closely linked with traditions from southern Jordan (see Section 4.2), and appearing to serve a large southern Jordanian culturally affiliated population in the northeastern Negev (Beit-Arieh 1995a; Danielson 2020b: 122–127, 2022: 133–137).

The integration of these cooking pots – to varying degrees at varying sites – is best understood as relating to movement and cultural interaction. Notably, the sites with the greatest culinary diversity were located on the major east-west road from Edom to the Mediterranean. At these sites, diversity and its integration are attested even in individual domestic contexts, as seen at the fort of Horvat ʿUza. Further, when textual descriptions and artistic depictions of food preparation are considered, it is possible to associate this activity with persons of a lesser perceived social status, including women, as a part of the broader household economy (Gero and Conkey 1991; Ebeling 2010; Peters 2016: 69–81).[14] In this way, it is possible that degrees of culinary diversity as seen in a military fort garrisoned by Judahite male soldiers, was perhaps the result of social alliances created through intermarriage, or the result of prisoners of war or enslaved people holding to specific culinary traditions. Notably, reference to trade in humans is preserved in the Hebrew Bible, where texts set in the eighth century BCE record the transfer of forcibly "exiled communities" between Gaza and Edom (Amos 1:6–12),[15] with the road connecting these regions traveling directly past these sites in the northeastern Negev. As outlined in Section 3, the roles played by trade and pastoralism underscore how the region was inherently linked to mobility and movement, modes by which we might expect evidence of culinary diversity.

4.1.2 Food Consumption and Iconic Tableware Traditions

Beyond food preparation and the vessels involved, we can also focus on the practice of food consumption and related tableware assemblages. Local tableware of the northeastern Negev is largely undecorated (Figure 15A), and can be contrasted with a diverse and often decorated tableware assemblage common to southern Jordan, which also extends selectively to certain locations in the northeastern Negev. This tableware is known as "Southern Transjordan-Negev Pottery", or "Busayra Painted Ware" (BPW) after one of its earliest and most prominent contexts of discovery (Figure 15B). At Busayra, vast amounts of this ware were excavated atop the acropolis in the vicinity of the palatial and temple complexes (Bienkowski 2002b). The corpus of BPW consists predominantly of bowls and kraters – forms used in the presentation and consumption of food – and stands out for its distinctive painted patterns and motifs, consisting of ladder, triangle, net, triglyph, and metopes applied in black, brown, red and white colors (Thareani 2010; Tebes 2011b;

---

[14]   In relation to texts from the Hebrew Bible that mention food production see Job 31:10; 1 Samuel 8:13, 28:24; 2 Samuel 11:21, 13:8; Leviticus 26:26; Exodus 11:5; Judges 9:53; Lamentations 4:10.

[15]   The enslavement and selling of people was common in this region at this time (e.g., Exodus 21:1–11; Deuteronomy 15:12). Consider also later regional evidence of enslaved persons from the fifth and fourth centuries BCE (Gropp 2001: WDSP 2, 9).

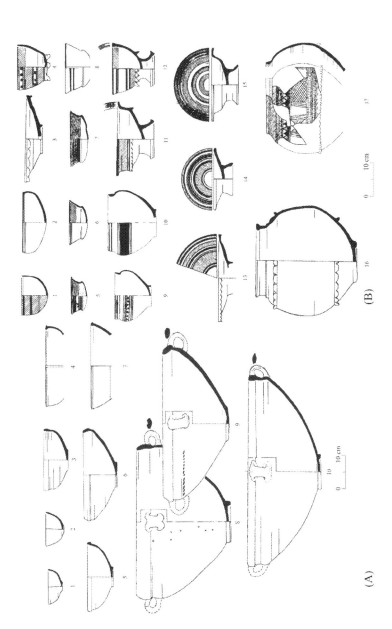

Figure 15 (A) Tableware common in the northeastern Negev of southern Judah (figure adapted from Beit-Arieh and Freud 2015: pls. 3.4.1, 3.4.3); (B) examples of Busayra Painted Ware (BPW; Figure adapted from Bienkowski 2002b: Figs. 9.1, 9.2, 9.5, 9.7, 9.25, 9.26, 9.29, 9.30; Cohen and Bernick-Greenberg 2007: Pl. 11.79: 12; Thareani 2010: Fig. 1; Beit-Arieh and Freud 2015: Pl. 3.4.1, 3.4.3; Freud 2015: Fig. 4.130)

Bienkowski 2015). This tableware is further marked as distinct from the northeastern Negev assemblage on the basis of form as well as the not-uncommon presence of plastic denticulations.

The iconic painted decorations of the BPW corpus, as found through southern Jordan, appear to follow a northwest Arabian tradition. Indeed, at each of the major oasis sites to the south of Edom (e.g., Tayma, Dedan, Qurayyah, etc.), iconic decorative patterns mark the pottery – and tableware – as distinct (Tebes 2013, 2015; Hausleiter 2014; Luciani and Alsaud 2018). The BPW corpus has also often been (mistakenly) identified as related to, or derivative of, Assyrian Palace Ware (APW) and its southern Levantine adaptations and imitations. While the BPW corpus does include some APW *forms*, these selections are part of a much broader formal repertoire, with the imitative APW forms fully indigenized through their decorative motifs (Brown 2018a). Further, this decorated assemblage is neither homogenous, nor linked to a single locale of production (Iserlis and Thareani 2011), yet the iconic decorations on them, particularly when contrasted with other non-decorative forms, stand out.

The consumption of food is inherently social, and tableware is necessary to facilitate dining. The consumption of food in groups creates situations in which social bonds are fostered or created anew, with the opportunity for performativity and the potential in these instances for material objects to serve a communicative role. Indeed, much anthropological literature has focused on the importance of communal consumption and feasts, highlighting them as contexts in which kinship or alliance relationships are fostered, obligations are created, and the aesthetics of distinction enforced (Fox and Harrell 2008; Pollock 2012; Altmann and Fu 2014). In such contexts, status inequalities, and demonstrations of opulence can serve as a means by which to create and replicate power (Dietler 2001; Bray 2003; Jiménez et al. 2011).

In contexts of performative commensality where social relationships and alliances are structured (Dietler 2001: 103–104), tableware can serve a subtle though key visual role. For example, it has been demonstrated in Near Eastern and analogous contexts that open areas with lowlight or firelight in which ritual feasting occurred, served to visually emphasize the elaborate decorations on serving vessels, highlighting their visual association with the performative aspects of feasts and the prestige of the hosts (Mills 2007; Porter 2011: 41–46). Thus, whether or not locations where BPW was used can be definitively identified with feasting, the highly iconic decorations would nonetheless serve as an indexical marker of the prestige of the ware, and the individuals and contexts associated with its use (Keane 2003). Moreover, through its semiotic association with elite commensality, when clusters of BPW are excavated in areas that can be linked to feasts, they may be understood as a form of political power (Kurtz 2001: 35–36).

The semiotic significance of such vessels is visible at the site of Busayra. Here, not only have the largest quantities of this decorated tableware been excavated, but also its most elaborate and highest quality versions. These wares have been found in significant quantities on the acropolis (Figure 16), with the vast majority excavated in Area B, between the palatial compound (Area C) and the temple complex (Area A; Bienkowski 2002b; Danielson 2020a: 172–176, 421). Of the limited available data related to foodways from the original excavations at the site, the faunal data from the acropolis has indicated a young age at slaughter for the most prevalent animal species: sheep (*Ovis aries*) and goat (*Capra hircus*; Bienkowski 2002a: 471–474). This culling pattern suggests that herd management strategies here were not wholly related to subsistence, but likely suggest elite consumption of prized (young) specimens. Moreover, the initial interpretations of the faunal data from the renewed excavations atop the acropolis have similarly confirmed this pattern, but also point to a higher-than-average culling of female sheep and goats, emphasizing the idea of conspicuous consumption in this space at Busayra (Brown 2018b: 117–121). While it is not possible to directly link the BPW tableware with the faunal data in a specific context indicating patterned feasts, the accumulation of this data atop the acropolis certainly points in the

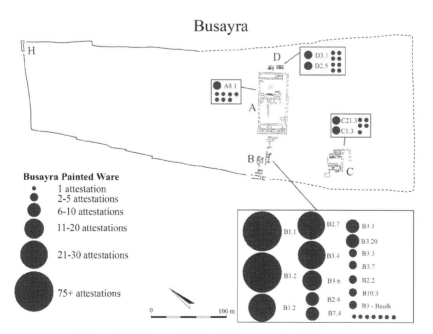

Figure 16 Busayra Painted Ware vessels at Busayra

direction that elite consumption in communal settings occurred, and that BPW was featured.

Elsewhere in Edom, clusters of BPW similarly appear, despite the paucity of excavation data from southern Jordan. At Tawilan, for example, BPW is found throughout the site, thoroughly integrated into diverse contexts (Bennett and Bienkowski 1995; Danielson 2020a: 176–179, 423). Further south, at Ghrareh, a site understood as the southernmost node of Edomite authority in the highlands, we similarly see clusters of this ware (Figure 17). Notably at Ghrareh, the BPW is clustered in the large central structure, interpreted as an elite residence (Hart 1988; Danielson 2020a: 181–183, 426). While faunal data from Ghrareh is lacking, these indications suggest communal consumption using BPW. Similarly, at Ghrareh Type CP4 cooking pots were most prominent (52 percent; $n = 45$), with Type CP6 as the second most common (30 percent; $n = 24$). Indeed, when mapped spatially, the distribution and clusters of BPW show their prominence at Busayra, with different clusters of the ware seemingly extending from Busayra to various nodes throughout the established trade network (Figure 18).

These wares are also attested to the west, throughout the northeastern Negev, though most prominently at Tel Malhata, Tel ʿAroer, and Horvat Qitmit, sites that demonstrate strong cultural links to southern Jordan. The locations where they

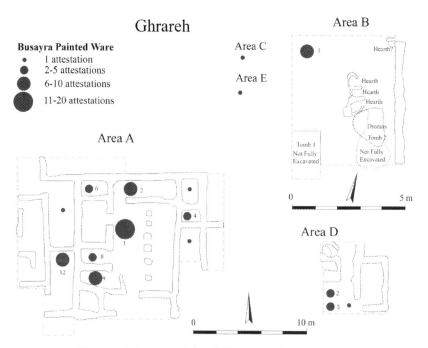

Figure 17 Busayra Painted Ware vessels at Ghrareh

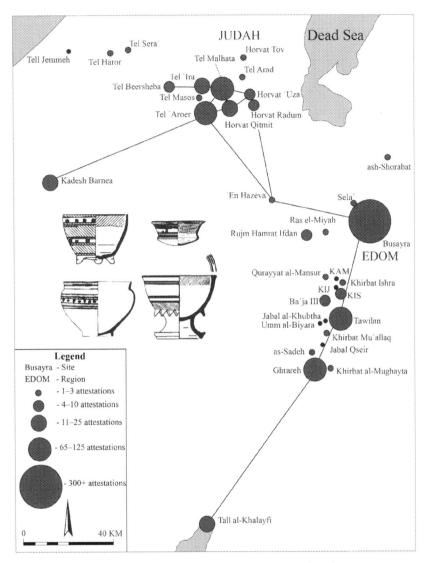

Figure 18 Regional distribution of Busayra Painted Ware

were excavated at Tel ʿAroer are particularly intriguing. Here, we first see that BPW was present already in the eighth century BCE (Stratum IV–III) and spread throughout the majority of the site (Figure 19; Danielson 2020a: 198–201). The prominence of the ware also appears to increase in the seventh century BCE (Stratum II), and while it is still found in all areas of the site, it is most strongly clustered in the extramural contexts of Area D and especially Area A, which was interpreted as a caravanserai (Thareani-Sussely 2007; Thareani 2010). In this caravanserai context, numerous other items associated with food preparation and

Tel ʿAroer (Strata IV-III)   Tel ʿAroer (Stratum II)

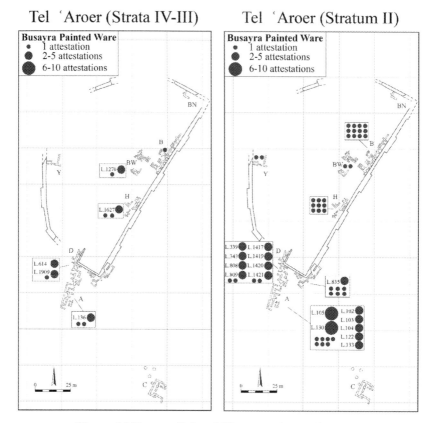

Figure 19 Busayra Painted Ware vessels at Tel ʿAroer

consumption have been identified (e.g., clay ovens, grinding stones, cooking pots). Likewise, amidst a broader program of herd management aimed toward secondary product exploitation, the limited faunal data – especially from the caravanserai – indicates a high percentage of animals culled in their first year, similar to Busayra, suggesting more conspicuous consumption (Motro 2011: 275–279; Thareani 2011: 115–178, 301–311).

To further complicate the picture of cross-cultural interaction in the northeastern Negev, while it might be assumed that tableware aligned with traditions in southern Jordan would be used to consume food prepared in a cooking pot common to southern Jordan (e.g., CP4), in the caravanserai at Tel ʿAroer this does not appear to have been the case. Rather, while several CP4 vessels were excavated here, the vast majority of cooking was done in CP2 vessels (Danielson 2020a: 198–201, 435–437), exemplifying a unique entanglement between diverse forms of food preparation and consumption. Similarly, the inverse situation is also attested. For example, at Horvat ʿUza, while a sizable minority of CP4 vessels were excavated, the nearly nonexistent examples of BPW at the site indicate this was not a recognizable form of food consumption at this site, or indeed at any of the other military forts of the region (Horvat Tov, Tel Arad, Horvat Radum).

Ultimately, the distribution of BPW reveals a shared practice of food consumption that was clearly centered on Busayra and emanates throughout southern Jordan and the northeastern Negev, particularly at nodal sites of the region's trade network. This is not necessarily reflective of an "ethnic" component, but rather reveals an association with prestige and status, echoing practices that are well attested in Edom. Furthermore, it is important to emphasize that similar to the petrographic and INAA analysis of CP4 vessels, BPW appears to have been produced in several major groups, one aligned with southern Jordan, and another with the northeastern Negev or northern Arabah (Gunneweg and Mommsen 1990, 1995; Gunneweg et al. 1991; Gunneweg and Balla 2002; Thareani 2010; Iserlis and Thareani 2011). This pattern appears to indicate different points of production, signifying that it was shared in specific elite contexts throughout the region. Lastly, similar to the cooking pot data, we can highlight both the longevity of this practice and its differential integration into sites in the region, suggesting unique narratives for different sites and different contexts.

4.2 Living with Gods in Contested Lands

Turning toward religious practice in the northeastern Negev, analyses have traditionally focused on the juxtaposition of two deities – Yahweh and Qos – and on an assumed homogenous religious orientation of Judah toward Yahweh, and Edom toward Qos. In particular, the discovery of the religious shrine at Horvat Qitmit, with its iconic religious artifacts and numerous inscriptions referencing Qos, has worked to highlight religious differences between Judah and Edom in the northeastern Negev (Beit-Arieh 1995a). While these deities were indeed singularly prominent in these regions, and despite the analytical expedience of such contrasts, this type of approach tends to essentialize the complexities of religious traditions and ritual behavior, highlighting and promoting the idea of homogenous singularities between cultural groups. Moreover, from another angle, this approach tends to reflect more the Deuteronomic orthodoxy as presented in the Hebrew Bible, rather than explaining the complexities of relationships between different deities and their adherents in this region. An alternative approach centers the house as the primary locus of religious activity (Smoak 2022) and then considers the effect of larger regional shrines and external temples. In the following discussion, patterns of religious practice are examined first at the household level, and subsequently at increasing geographic and social scales. Structuring the analysis in this way avoids the expedience of contrasting large-scale "cultural" groups, focusing instead on the realia of everyday religious life and the effect that different social structures or elite agents may have upon it.

Recent scholarship on the archaeology of religion and the household has emphasized its embeddedness in everyday life, and the inability of modernist thought to necessarily understand its nuances (Edwards 2005; Nakhai 2014; Zevit 2014). Deities and the supernatural were indeed an integral and real component of the landscape and communication with or reaction to them was not separate from everyday activities (Stowers 2008: 8–9). As such, many of these practices would likely not have been recognized by their performers as a separate class of "religious" activity, but rather merely the status quo of what life entailed when the divine was a constant in the physical world. It is difficult then, and perhaps inappropriate to a degree, to identify some material culture as "religious" and others as not since it all held the potential for use in religious activity. Nonetheless, in focusing on individual household structures, it is possible to highlight areas where ritual activity can be most easily identified according to modernist understandings, and to examine the associated material culture (Daviau 2001; Bodel and Olyan 2008; Albertz and Schmitt 2012; Albertz et al. 2014). The objects from such contexts most commonly identified with household religion include altars, stands, zoomorphic or anthropomorphic figurines (including Judean Pillar Figurines; hereafter JPFs), specialized vessels, as well as a variety of unmarked objects, or faunal remains, whose use would be dependent on local beliefs, ritual requirements, and the availability of resources (Daviau 2012; Nakhai 2014: 57).

At Tel 'Ira, for example, a variety of material culture traditionally associated with household religion was excavated, including two small incense altars and numerous figurines (Beck 1999; Goldsmith et al. 1999: 469–470; Kletter 1999). One of the altars was excavated in a room of the casemate wall system (Room/Locus 191) that also contained a variety of domestic ceramics including seven bowls (including one BPW), three kraters, three cooking pots (types CP12 and CP14), two juglets, four lamps, two jars, a flask, and a JPF (Freud 1999: 262–263; Kletter 1999: 375, No. 4). The figurine assemblage is largely of the JPF variety, with additional zoomorphic figurines, and apart from several fill or surface finds, the remainder were excavated in domestic contexts. Several variant figurines were also excavated, one from an anthropomorphic vessel in a domestic context (Kletter 1999: 376, 384, No. 7), and another fragment of a female figurine that appears to have formerly been applied to a cultic stand-type vessel (Kletter 1999: 375, 384, No. 8). Somewhat divergent stylistically from this assemblage was an anthropomorphic plaque that bore both male and female genitalia and held a tambourine, whose closest stylistic parallels are at Horvat Qitmit, Tel Malhata, and in Transjordan (Beck 1999; Kletter 1999: 375, 2015: 548).

Nearby at Tel Masos, the late Iron Age contexts from Area G similarly emphasize the integration of ritual activity into everyday life. In Room 708, a context that appears linked with food preparation, the excavated material culture remains included four cooking pots (Type CP1), a bowl, juglets, a storejar, two lamps, and the base of a JPF (Albertz and Schmitt 2012: 130–131). Additional figurine (JPF) fragments were found in areas where there were no indications of formal domestic shrines or ritual spaces, indicating that ritual activity was embedded in domestic life.

Shifting focus regionally to southern Jordan, the site of Tawilan provides some intriguing similarities. First, the areas of the site that have been excavated appear to indicate primarily domestic residences in an agropastoral subsistence-based village (Bennett and Bienkowski 1995: 103–105). Moreover, the distribution of material culture remains relating to domestic activities is spread throughout the site, indicating that while some variances in the organization of household activities between different kin groups are likely, overall aspects of domestic life were relatively evenly patterned (Brown 2018b: 89–92). Figurine fragments, traditionally associated with ritual, were found in greater quantities in Area III to the west, an area also associated with food and textile production (Brown 2018b: 91, 190–192; Danielson 2020a: 307, 422–423). Two additional small altars were found in other domestic contexts. It is difficult to identify any specific deities or practices, or ways that material culture indicators of "religion" could be isolated to particular areas of the site. Rather, Tawilan demonstrates that interaction with the divine could not be separated from the everyday contexts, especially in cooking and textile production areas.

In the more culturally diverse towns of Tel 'Aroer and Tel Malhata, similar patterns are present. At Tel 'Aroer all the ritual material culture derives from domestic or nonformal ritual contexts, integrated with items of everyday use (Danielson 2020a: 299–300). As one example, in Locus 339 in a small room in Area D west, a JPF was excavated with a zoomorphic figurine, bowls (including BPW), a cooking pot (Type CP2), a seal with a bull head and two spatulas (Thareani 2011: 86, Pl. 125). These contexts do well to illustrate the integration of ritual acts in the everyday acts of cooking and weaving, but also to highlight the entangled culinary traditions previously described. In the intramural context of Locus 1621 in Area H, a zoomorphic vessel, a fragment of a kernos, two rattles, a spatula, and a jar stopper were excavated. This context was interpreted as a rubbish depository, and based on the nature of the finds, may suggest they came from a more formalized ritual space in the domestic structure (Thareani 2011: 107, Pl. 177).

Tel Malhata presents further insights. First, five stone altars were excavated in Pillared Building 1564 in Area H (Stratum IIIA), with three of the altars clustered together in the southwest corner of the room together with wooden furniture, bone inlays, and a 23 cm long phallus-shaped clay object (Beit-Arieh 2015; Freud and Reshef 2015: 591). The size of the structure and the nature and clustering of the finds suggest that this corner may have served a more formalized ritual purpose, perhaps associated with food preparation and the textile industry operating in the surrounding rooms, at a level above that of a single household (Schmitt 2014: 270–271; Koch and Sapir-Hen 2018: 435). Regarding the remainder of the ritual artifact assemblage, particularly figurines, we find them present and integrated into the everyday contexts and activities of different households, though few JPFs have been excavated (Danielson 2020a: 304–306). What is particularly intriguing, however, is that while they depict elements that would be considered common in a "Judahite" assemblage (e.g., females, horses), they are created in a technological style that is more commonly seen in southern Jordan than the Negev. Other examples present additional stylistic features ("grotesque" style heads) or present females in the plaque style similar to Busayra, but with some unique features (Sedman 2002: 375–376; Kletter 2015: 572).

Ultimately, all of these contexts demonstrate the rootedness of ritual practice in everyday life and domestic contexts. In creating a typology of ritual spaces for the southern Levant, Rüdiger Schmitt has categorized these domestic spaces as of two types, one relating to religious practice that is wholly integrated with everyday activity, often in contexts of food or textile production, and a second, where a more formalized space in a house (corner, bench, rooftop, etc.) is the location of a cluster of specialized objects (Schmitt 2014: 267–269). What all of these sites highlight, however, is that the human practices associated with household religion are highly similar across the broader region. While figurines may have been made with slightly different technologies or appear in slightly different styles (Sedman 2002; Kletter 2015), the *function* and *use* of these objects suggest similar practices. Such a similarity can be seen more broadly as well, where the categories of objects and their locations of use suggest similar patterns, despite the potential that they were oriented toward different deities or aligned with different ideologies.

The deities to whom this ritual activity in the household was directed are not entirely clear. Certainly, Yahweh and Qos were well known and perhaps revered in the household, but more compellingly, the prevalence of female figurines (e.g., JPFs), suggests potentially a physical model of a female deity, or more likely apotropaic practice or supplications toward a female deity (Kletter 1996; Darby 2014; Dever 2014). Often associated with Asherah, this common practice in the house likely centered on a goddess who may have also been identified as a consort of Yahweh or Qos. In viewing this data then, the strongest evidence of a deity in the material culture of the house features neither Yahweh nor Qos.

Religious practice, however, did not cease at the household level. While the house was undoubtedly the most frequented religious space, larger, regional, and community ritual spaces played an important role, and it is in these spaces that starker differences in practice are identified.

At the community or regional scale, the site of Horvat Qitmit was the most prominent religious site in the northeastern Negev. Located in the south-central portion of the Beersheba-Arad Valley, it was visible to nearly every major site in the region. Horvat Qitmit consisted of two structure complexes and several stone enclosures. Complex A consisted of a rectangular structure at its northern end that contained three parallel rooms, each measuring approximately 2 × 4 m (Figure 20A). Each room contained a bench along its east wall, and at a right angle to the entrance of each room, a wall appeared to function as a podium or table (Beit-Arieh 1995a: 9–12). In the structure, substantial amounts of pottery and animal bones, as well as several figurines were excavated, with evidence that the rooms were periodically cleaned, perhaps making use of a favissa (Beit-Arieh 1995a: 12–13, 26). To the south was an open-air space with a raised stone platform, interpreted as a *bāmāh*, surrounded by a stone enclosure wall. To the east of this delineated space was a poorly preserved small wall surrounding a flint-slab-topped altar, a round basin, and a small pit (Beit-Arieh 1995a: 13–20).

Complex B at Horvat Qitmit was located approximately 15 m to the north of Complex A and consisted of a square-shaped structure measuring 8 × 8.5 m (Figure 20B). Several rooms were located on the west, north, and northeast sides, surrounding an open-air courtyard. A small standing stone, interpreted as a *maṣṣēbah* was excavated here, with significant evidence in the complex for food preparation (Beit-Arieh 1995a: 20–24). At Horvat Qitmit, Type CP4 cooking pots accounted for the overwhelming majority of types, and significant amounts of BPW were similarly excavated. Two additional stone enclosures, consisting of delineated elliptical spaces with only a single surviving course of stones in its wall, were also uncovered. Their purpose is not entirely clear, but they may have functioned as animal enclosures or served an unknown ritual function (Beit-Arieh 1995a: 24–26).

Horvat Qitmit is best known, however, for its iconic statuary and its association with the god Qos. Numerous fragmentary inscriptions preserve the name Qos, suggesting this deity to have been an important focus at the site, though not the sole deity (Beit-Arieh 1995b). The head of a horned goddess was also excavated and was likely a prominently featured deity (Figure 20C). Further, the tripartite division of Complex A suggests that a third deity may also have been present. Numerous other anthropomorphic figures likely representing priests or worshippers were excavated (Figure 20D), together with male,

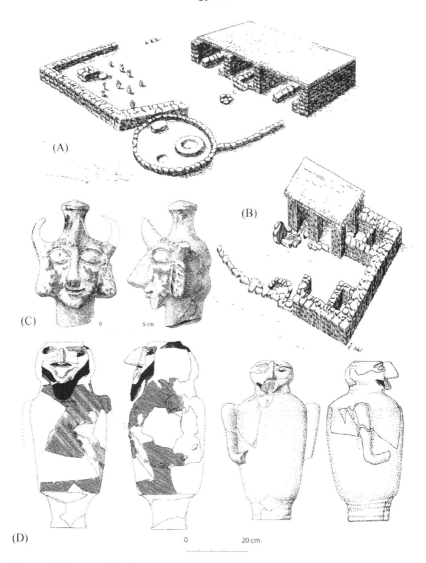

Figure 20 Horvat Qitmit: (A) reconstruction of Complex A; (B) reconstruction
of Complex B; (C) head of female deity; (D) anthropomorphic male
figures (figures after Beit-Arieh 1995a: Fig. 9.1, 9.2; Beck 1995:
figs. 3.17, 3.19, 3.22, 3.23, 3.53, 3.54)

female, and zoomorphic figurines, as well as a sphynx, musical instruments,
architectural stands with human, floral, and pomegranate decorative features
(Beck 1995). Notably, the assemblage appears divergent from what has been
excavated elsewhere in Judah, with stronger influences associated with central
and southern Jordan. Together with the association of Qos to southern Jordan,

Horvat Qitmit has been compellingly argued as related to the cultural and religious practices common in Edom and particularly among the elite of Edom.

Due to its location along the east-west road, Horvat Qitmit has long been interpreted as a wayside shrine for diverse groups moving through the region (Finkelstein 1992). However, petrographic and INAA studies on material from Qitmit have also identified a local signature for ceramic production (Gunneweg and Mommsen 1995; Freud 2014). In other words, the material culture was produced in the environs of the northeastern Negev, and thus the site was also frequented by people local to the region. Similarly, further research on the material culture from Tel Malhata has identified strong similarities that indicate a close relationship between the two nearby sites, beginning by at least the early seventh century BCE (Tel Malhata Stratum IIIB; Beit-Arieh, Freud and Tal 2015: 742). In this way, Horvat Qitmit must be viewed as an inherently local feature of the religious landscape, and at home in the northeastern Negev. The fact that Horvat Qitmit stood in this region for approximately a century without evidence of hostility or even destruction at the time of its abandonment, demonstrates that the site was not viewed in an overly negative way by the inhabitants of the region, or presumably the Judahite administration whose fortresses were scattered throughout the valley.

On the highway to the east, at the northern end of the Arabah Valley and adjacent to the fort at ʿEn Hazeva, is an additional space of broader community religious significance. The religious space is unfortunately poorly preserved and yet awaits its final publication, but appears to consist of a small rectilinear U-shaped structure interpreted as a shrine (Cohen and Yisrael 1995, 1996). From a nearby favissa dug near the fortress walls, a significant number of iconic ritual artifacts were excavated, including anthropomorphic and non-anthropomorphic stands, altars, pedestalled bowl incense burners, chalices, perforated tripod cup incense burners, incense shovels, bowls, and pomegranates (Cohen and Yisrael 1995: 224–225). While no deity can be explicitly identified from the assemblage, the similarity of the artifacts to Horvat Qitmit and southern Jordan, with the discovery of an incised goring bull suggesting a weather deity, has led to the suggestion that here too, Qos was the primary deity of focus (Beck 1996).

It would be tempting to contrast the apparent singularity of Horvat Qitmit in the northeastern Negev (and nearby ʿEn Hazeva), with the famed temple located at Tel Arad. There, a small tripartite temple measuring 12 × 18 m was excavated (Herzog 2002), whose character and association with the Judahite administration compellingly suggest Yahweh was the deity of focus. However, two factors prevent the religious practices at the Tel Arad temple from being compared to those at Horvat Qitmit. First, and most glaringly, is the fact that the small Tel

Arad temple was decommissioned in the late eighth century BCE, prior to the construction of Horvat Qitmit (Herzog 2002: 14, 49–50). Thus, the temple at Tel Arad and the sanctuary at Horvat Qitmit did not exist at the same time. Second, is the fact that as an intramural temple in a military fort, its public accessibility is in question. Similarly, a larger, formal religious space has been determined to have existed at Tel Beersheba, though again, this space was decommissioned prior to the end of the eighth century BCE, and thus was not contemporary with Horvat Qitmit (Zevit 2001: 171, 301–302).

Beyond, we are confronted with the larger state-promoted religious centers of Judah and Edom that were both nearly equidistant from the northeastern Negev. At Jerusalem was a large temple linked to Yahweh (and a consort?) that was constructed and promoted by the ruling elite (Bloch-Smith 2002; Lemaire 2011). Similarly, at Busayra, adjacent to the palatial center was a large temple complex oriented toward Qos (and a consort?),[16] with its close proximity to the palace demonstrating its entangled relationship with the ruling elite, similar to Jerusalem (Bienkowski 2002a: 94–95; Porter 2004: 381–387). It is difficult, however, to gauge the impact that these somewhat distant ($\approx$ 70 km) "state" religious centers had on the northeastern Negev. The relation between household ritual and larger state sanctuaries has been argued to have been somewhat mutually influential (Albertz and Schmitt 2012: 55). However, the state and its sanctioned religion can also function as "top-down" movement that can push for particular patterns of religious practice, as seen for example in the promotion of the Deuteronomistic ideals (Deuteronomy 12; 2 Kings 22–23). Thus, through conformity and centralization, such promoted religion can benefit the elite through increased sociopolitical control and wealth creation (Meyers 2012: 166–168).

A further mode by which to track the popularity of the state-promoted deities is through naming practices and the custom of adding part of a deity name – a theophoric element – to one's own. For Yahweh, this involves the addition of יהו (*yhw*), and for Qos, קוס (*qws*). Previous scholarship has established the popularity of Yahwistic elements in Judah, and Qos elements with Edom, which are well reflected in the naming practices of their kings in the late Iron Age (e.g., *ḥzqyhw*, *ṣdqyhw* of Judah vs. *qwsmlk* and *qwsgbr* of Edom; Bartlett 1989: 200–207; Golub 2014, 2017; Sanders 2015; Danielson 2020b, 2022: 137–140). Such names cannot immediately be taken to indicate the religious preferences or practices of individuals, but they do identify trends, and when clustered together spatially and chronologically, can yield insights

---

[16] There is no explicit evidence that Qos was the primary deity at Busayra, though all circumstantial evidence indicates such (Danielson 2020b: 119–127; Danielson et al. 2022: 5–8).

into the ideologies of different communities (Zadok 1997; Aldrin 2016; Nyström 2016). Owing to the rich inscriptional record of the northeastern Negev, it is possible to examine onomastic trends by site and diachronically, while noting that this dataset is both androcentric and reflective of the Judahite administration.

Several trends become apparent when compiling the onomastic data from the northeastern Negev and Edom (Figure 21A).[17] First, while Yahwistic and Qos names are dominant among the Judahite and Edomite kings respectively, they are not ubiquitous. Nevertheless, the general prominence of these deities in these regions is evident. In fact, Qos names are not at all well-attested at Judahite administrative sites (e.g., Horvat ʿUza; Tel Arad, Tel ʿIra). Nor are Yahwistic names well attested at southern Jordanian or Edomite-administered sites (e.g., Tall al-Khalayfi). Moreover, little overlap between Yahwistic and Qos names is seen at any site, with the only reference to Qos names at Tel Arad referencing persons from outside Arad.[18] Among the general corpus, numerous references to El (אל) are also present, although this deity name could be used in its generic sense ("god") and thus relate to either Yahweh or Qos. With regard to the major "towns" in the region, however, this pattern is not emulated. Intriguingly, Tel Malhata, the site with perhaps the greatest diversity seen in the previous discussion, bears no evidence for Yahwistic or Qos names, though the dataset is limited (n=12). Similarly, at Tel ʿAroer, there is evidence for a Qos name though the dataset is even more limited.

While the overall dataset is skewed toward the military administrative forts of Horvat ʿUza and Tel Arad, these two sites nonetheless evidence a strong association with Yahwistic names. Moreover, through this richer dataset it is possible to examine patterns in naming practices over multiple generations as many of the administrative lists excavated there preserve the patronyms of individuals. Thus, focusing on the names that identify two generations, we can detect a relative degree of stability in Yahwistic names at Arad, while at Horvat ʿUza there is a rapid increase in Yahwistic names in the second generation (Figure 21B). It is possible that the rapid increase in Yahwistic names at Horvat ʿUza relates to the fort's history. While Tel Arad had existed in the northeastern Negev for centuries, Horvat ʿUza was not established until the seventh century BCE (Table 1; Herzog 2002: 14; Beit-Arieh 2007b). As such, it would have required a large population influx in order to build and garrison the

---

[17] For a compiled list of all of these names, see Danielson (2020a: 413–418).

[18] It is possible that the reconstructed name [*qw*]*s ʿnl* from Tel Arad (Aharoni 1981: 26) refers to the same administrator referenced in the inscriptions at Tall al-Khalayfi (Divito 1993: 53–55). If this were the same individual, then it is a highly intriguing example of cooperation by two individuals in separate administrations (Danielson 2020a: 370–372).

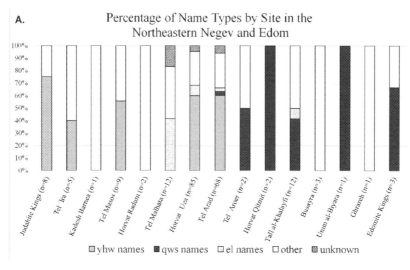

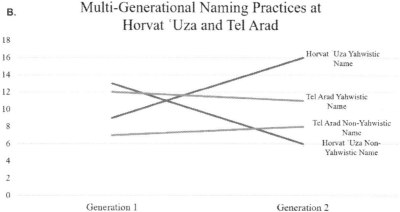

Figure 21 (A) Percentage of onomastic types by site in the northeastern
Negev and Edom; and (B) multigenerational naming practices at Horvat
'Uza and Tel Arad

fort. It is possible that this influx of persons held ties to the Jerusalem region,
where naming practices may have been patterned after Yahweh more rigidly
than in the northeastern Negev.

To summarize, the preceding discussion has highlighted the complexities of
describing religious practices that can be evidenced at a variety of social scales
and through different datasets. While there are indeed differences that determine certain communities to have been more closely aligned with Yahweh and
others with Qos, as suggested by the onomastic data, this is only part of the
story. On the basis of household data, despite slight differences in the stylistic or

technological manufacture of figurines, the *practices* and *use* of these objects in domestic contexts appear to have been shared throughout the region. It is not possible to identify specific deities of focus in such a setting, other than the preponderance of female figurines, which, if indeed linked with a female deity through their apotropaic function, could be aligned with either Yahweh or Qos as an association with a consort is likely for both. This is not to say that domestic religion was necessarily identical throughout southern Jordan and the north-eastern Negev, but rather that the rituals and practices would likely have been recognizable and cross-culturally understood. In fact, if one is to delve into textual and inscriptional data, it appears likely that numerous ritual customs were shared throughout Judah and Edom, seemingly including male circumcision (Jeremiah 9:25–26) and the offering of unleavened bread (Ahituv 2008: 354).

The commonalities of practice amidst the prominence of different deities in different regions likely relate to the rootedness of the gods in the landscape. In other words, certain gods were more closely linked with particular landscapes, and perhaps variant manifestations of the same deity could be identified at various locales in that landscape. Thus, transitioning from a focus on one god to another between different geographic or social settings, may not have been particularly remarkable to ancient persons migrating to a new context or marrying into a new social group (McCarter 1987: 140–141; Smith 2016: 91–92; Miller 2021: 88). Such examples are known in migration contexts in the ancient world, where syncretism will occur between a traditional god and those dominant in a new context (Winnicki 2009: 300, 303; Danielson 2020b: 162–170). The question remains then, as to what degree this household practice reflected, and/or influenced larger patterns of collective religious activity (Albertz and Schmitt 2012: 55; Sanders 2015)

Starker differences do appear at broader social scales. In the northeastern Negev during the seventh and sixth centuries BCE, Horvat Qitmit was domin-ant, in part due to its central location, but also due to the fact that there were no other regional shrines or temples with which to compete. Its focus on the deity Qos, and at least one other unnamed female deity, would have been common knowledge in the region. The culinary and other material culture evidence from Horvat Qitmit suggests that the shrine was not frequented by all social groups of the northeastern Negev. And yet, its existence does not appear to have been overly offensive to others, as, despite serving a minority of the population, the shrine was not damaged or destroyed during the approximate century of its use. This may very likely indicate that Qos was at home in this landscape. Even if one's family ideology was more aligned with the Deuteronomistic ideals that promoted Yahweh in Jerusalem, it is unlikely that many of the individuals or families in the region frequented or even saw the temple in Jerusalem.

Inadvertently, they would be far more visually familiar with the site of Horvat Qitmit upon its visible hill than the temple in Jerusalem. In this way, Horvat Qitmit and Qos may not have been viewed as foreign or intrusive, but merely different.

4.3 Foreign Accents and Scribal Power

Language and dialect differences form a significant and readily identifiable feature by which humans identify others as belonging to a specific community or as distinct from it. By all accounts, the language or dialect spoken in Edom was mutually intelligible with its immediate surrounding regions: Moab to the north, and Judah to the northwest. Isolating and determining linguistic variances between these regions is notoriously difficult. This is due in part to the method-ical challenges of solely using written inscriptions since we cannot access speakers from these ancient speech communities, but also because we have so few excavated inscriptions from Edom. Nonetheless, certain features from the limited inscriptional corpus do allow for a view into the speech practices in Edom and their relation to Judah, revealing a close similarity between them.[19]

For example, inscriptions associated with Edom make use of the definite article *hê-* (ה), which together with the use of the lexeme *bn* (בן), places this dialect as distinct from Aramaic and in the family tree of Canaanite. Further, the use of the relative pronoun *'šr* (אשר), and the accusative marker *'t* (את) high-lights a similarity with the neighboring languages spoken in Judah and Moab (Garr 1985: 228–230; Vanderhooft 1995; Rollston 2014). Significantly, the present dataset from Edom does not preserve any identifiable phonological features that would mark speech in Edom as overly distinctive from neighboring regions. Thus, on the basis of current data, it is possible to state that the languages spoken in both ancient Judah and ancient Edom were mutually intelligible, and are likely best described as variant dialects of a broader "south-ern Levantine" language (Garr 1985: 228–230; Segert 1997).

Identifying broad similarities in the spoken language, however, is not meant to indicate that differences would have been entirely absent, nor were they unnoticed. Humans possess the unique ability to identify even minute variances in speech or writing, using this to determine closeness with or distance from others (Jaffe et al. 2012; Sebba et al. 2012). As the Negev and southern Jordan relate to distinct topographical zones, whose inhabitants were predominantly engaged in subsistence practices, it is to be expected that regional pronunci-ations and phonological stresses, not to mention slang or slurs, would develop

---

[19] For a list of inscriptions and linguistic features that have been associated with Edom, see Danielson (2020a: Appendix C, D).

and perpetuate. This has been well documented in modern historical contexts (Nielsen 2005; Weldon 2018), and is also identifiable for the ancient world (Garr 1985; Colvin 2010). Such features would not necessarily be captured in writing, but would very much form a significant component in signaling distinctions between groups. Associating this principle with the southern Levant then, an individual from Tel ʿIra or Horvat Tov would likely be readily able to recognize differences in the speech of someone from Ghrareh or Tawilan, notwithstanding other highly indexical visual cues like dress or hair-style, which the statuary from Horvat Qitmit certainly suggests.

The oft-referenced *shibboleth* narrative from the Hebrew Bible well illus-trates this principle of identifying differences on the basis of speech:

> Then the Gileadites took the fords of Jordan against the Ephraimites. Whenever one of the fugitives of Ephraim said, "Let me go over," the men of Gilead would say to him, "Are you an Ephraimite?" When he said, "No," they said to him, "Then say Shibboleth" and he said "Sibboleth," for he could not pronounce it right. Then they seized him and killed him at the fords of the Jordan. Forty-two thousand of the Ephraimites fell at that time (Judges 12:5–6).

The text, in a gruesome manner, highlights the ease with which people can identify variances in speech, and notably the differences recounted here would not be preserved in the Iron Age writing system. Moreover, as this text derives from the first millennium BCE southern Levant, it not only preserves the idea of the ability to identify others on the basis of speech, but through its writing/recitation in its ancient context would have served to reinforce such stereotypes. In this instance, a rather minute and superficial marker of difference was, through narrative, emphasized as the means by which to identify and then enact violence on a neighboring group.

While it can be difficult to detect variances in speech in ancient written sources, certain inscriptions from the northeastern Negev do allow for such insight. For example, in the administrative texts of the Judahite garrison at Tel Arad, and attested elsewhere in Judahite administrative contexts, the phrase: "I bless you by *Yhwh*" (ברכתך ליהוה) is common (Aharoni 1981: nos. 16, 21, 40). In contrast, from the corpus at Horvat ʿUza, in an inscription identified as relating to Edom, the greeting/blessing formula is slightly different: "I bless you by *Qws*" (הברכתך לקוס; Beit-Arieh 2007a: No. 7). While at a certain level contrasts may be drawn between the deities that are the focus of the blessing, deeper differences exist at the linguistic level. English translations are unable to capture the nuance, but in the former, the verb in rendered in the D stem (*piʿēl*), whereas the latter uses the causative H stem (*hipʿîl*). Differences here then, are noted not only in the spelling and nuance of the verb, but also in the pronunciation. Thus, in these mutually intelligible greeting

formulae, while the variant deities draw a contrast, these differences are accentuated in the variant pronunciations and subtle nuances in the meaning of the
greeting/blessing verbs. It is worth emphasizing that this inscription was excavated
at the site of Horvat ʿUza, in the midst of these cross-cultural interactions.

The emphasis on regionalisms and their preservation of nuance can also be
extended to script. Just as "Edomite" and "Judahite" are problematic descriptions for a language that was mutually comprehensible, so too understandings of
script differences as relating to "national" scripts likely overstate the situation.
Certain differences in the script do exist. Inscriptions associated with the region
of Edom show strong similarities to Moab and Ammon, bearing sufficient
similarity to the contemporary Aramaic script to suggest a lack of early scribal
influence from Judah (Vanderhooft 1995; Rollston 2014).[20] In particular, we
can highlight the paleographic features of the letters *bêt*, *wāw*, *sāmek*, *ʿayin*,
qôp, *rêš*, and *tāw* that show an affinity with Aramaic, and the *dālet*, *hê*, and
alternate *sāmek* that appear to be unique to scribal practices in Edom
(Vanderhooft 1995; Rollston 2014).[21]

While such regional variances are identifiable, the extremely low literacy
rates of the ancient world, combined with the challenges of understanding
these kingdoms as "nations," indicates the labeling of these differences as
"national scripts" to be imprecise. Rather, as the overwhelming majority of
writing took place under the aegis of political and/or religious institutions by
a limited number of scribes, scribal differences instead seem to be the result of
different training that was perpetuated through generations of scribes
(Schniedewind 2013: 100–115, 117–120, 2019). While scribal variations
were indeed identifiable, they would have been recognized most readily
only by a limited number of literate persons, namely those associated with
the political administration.

In summary, the differences in speech between Judah and Edom that intersected in the northeastern Negev appear to have been largely superficial with the
language mutually intelligible. And yet, differences would have been readily
identifiable: in pronunciations, phonological stresses, and to a degree, formalized in standard greetings and blessings. Whether the outcome of determining
these variances in speech was benevolence, ambiguity, or hostility would
certainly vary by context, but the identification of such differences melds well
with the overall established tapestry of cross-cultural interactions and social
entanglements in the settlements of the northeastern Negev.

---

[20] Generally, provenance, reference to Qos, and paleography are used to associate inscriptions with
Edom, though this is an imperfect method of attribution (Vanderhooft 1995: 138–140).
[21] For a current list of script features associated with Edom see Danielson (2020a: Appendix E).

5 Memory and Mythmaking

You shall not abhor any of the Edomites, for they are your kin . . .
The children of the third generation that are born to them may be admitted to
the assembly of Yahweh.
(Deuteronomy 23:7–8, NRSV)

A discussion of cross-cultural interactions between Judah and Edom cannot be
complete without consideration of the textual traditions related to it. Much of the
history of scholarship of this region has been dominated by particular readings of
the biblical text that emphasize hostility, particularly on the part of Edom. Such
interpretations have focused on the curses and polemics against Edom that are
common in the prophetic and other literature (e.g., Isaiah 34, Amos 1:9–12,
Obadiah, Psalm 137, and Lamentations 4:21–22). However, while readily apparent
in the text, emphases on hostility and enmity represent only one characterization of
Edom. Just as with the archaeological record, the biblical tradition also contains
a multiplicity of perspectives, revealing different geographic, chronological, as well
as social, political, and religious perspectives of Edom. Disentangling these variant
thematic portrayals reveals a much more complex narrative. Similarly, situating the
biblical text as a product of the Judahite political and religious elite emphasizes its
position as an etic perspective toward both the Negev and Edom.

To begin, in Judah's bible, beyond the curses, Edom is described as autono-
mous, allocated to its inhabitants by Yahweh (Anderson 2011: 129–148), with its
so-called "Edomite King List" (Genesis 36) defining its position in the landscape
and in contrast to Judah (Nash 2018). The allocation of legitimacy to land on the
part of the biblical writers appears in numerous narratives, where the Israelites are
not permitted to travel through the land of Edom without consent (Deuteronomy
2:1–12; Numbers 20:14–21; Judges 11:14–18). Notably, in these instances, and
especially expressed in Deuteronomy 2:1–12, Edom is not condemned for its
unwillingness, but rather Yahweh explicitly acknowledges his gift of this region
to Edom and its legitimacy to it (Anderson 2011: 156–176; Fleming 2012: 84).
Thus, Edom's refusals, rather than being viewed as a form of hostility expressed
in the text, can instead be read as a recognition of legitimacy, and the right to
self-determination. Further, while Edom and Judah's neighbors – the people of
Moab and Ammon – are deemed by the Deuteronomist to be forever excluded
from the assembly of Yahweh, the people of Edom are among the few who are
offered conditional acceptance as a result of their shared kinship, as Edom is
Israel/Judah's brother (Deuteronomy 23:3–8; Tebes 2006b).[22]

---

[22] Within the biblical text there are numerous references and allusions to Edom. This work focusses
on select aspects of Edom as it appears in the prophetic corpus and the Pentateuch. For further
engagement with Edom as it appears in the narrative "histories" of Samuel and Kings, as well as

5.1 Legendary Patriarchs

The fraternal language used to describe Edom in the biblical text may relate in part to similar cultural practices, but more so as a result of the etiological narratives in Genesis. Here, while Judah's other neighbors, Ammon and Moab, are described as distantly related (first cousins once removed), with crude, incestuous false etymologies provided (Genesis 19:30–38), Edom is described as much more closely related – as a brother (e.g., Genesis 25: 19–34; 27; 35:29; Numbers 20:14; Deuteronomy 2:4, 8; 23:7; Amos 1:11; Obadiah 1:10, 12; Malachi 1:2–4; Assis 2006: 9). These kinship terms are exemplified in the patriarchal narratives where the legendary figures of Jacob and Esau – twin brothers – are cast as the ancestors of Israel/Judah and Edom respectively (Genesis 25, 27, 32–33; Blum 2012). In this portrayal, as often with kin, it is the relationship that takes precedence over grievances and wrongdoing.

The general trajectory of the Jacob-Esau narrative begins with the younger twin, Jacob, duping his elder brother Esau into selling his "birthright" for a pot of stew (as described previously in Section 4.1). With the help of his mother Rebekah, Jacob then deceives his father Isaac into giving him said birthright (Genesis 25, 27), seeming to begin to fulfill the prophesy surrounding his and Esau's birth, that Jacob would have dominance over his elder brother (Genesis 25:23). After fleeing Esau's fury, Jacob, after a period of time and yet in fear, returns with his family to make amends with Esau. Ultimately, Esau greets him warmly and their fraternal bonds are re-established (Genesis 32–33; Blum 2012). Throughout the narrative, both explicit and implicit references work to identify Jacob as the ancestor of Israel/Judah, and Esau as the ancestor of Edom. These references include the folk etymology of Esau's name as "hairy," or relating to the "hairy" or forested landscape of Seir in Edom, and numerous insinuations of Esau as "red" and eating "red stew." Here, the emphasis on red corresponds to the meaning of Edom as "red," and associates Esau with the iconic red sandstone formations of southwestern Jordan (Bartlett 1992; Knauf 1992a). While the folk etymology of Esau as "hairy" (Genesis 25:24–26) is not linguistically correct (Hendel 1987: 111), it nonetheless serves to situate him in a landscape that would be moderately familiar to the reader. Such etymological associations follow a similar Hebrew Bible and broader ancient Near Eastern practice of connecting epic characters to social groupings, tribes, or polities (Hendel 1987: 113–115).

The narrative trajectory of the broader Jacob Cycle, however, likely already represents the weaving together of several traditions. Namely, the Jacob-Esau

---

the formation and complexities of these texts, see Crowell (2021: 177–218), Germany (2022) and Bartlett (1995).

narratives (Genesis 25–27) likely stood as an independent tradition from the Jacob-Laban narratives (Genesis 29–31), one oriented toward the south, and the other to the north (Hensel 2021b). These differences and a complex redaction history are evidenced by their variant structure, geographic locations, and contradictions between the texts (Schmid 2021; Wöhrle 2021). On the basis of this complexity, a fruitful way to consider these narratives, and of the ways by which meaning may be drawn from them, is through the lens of cultural memory, following Halbwach's (1992) ideas of collective memory (Hendel 2010). By highlighting the ideas of cultural memory, we can reconcile the deep past setting of the patriarchal narratives with their composition and redactions in the mid first millennium BCE (Finkelstein and Römer 2014; Hensel 2021c). In doing so, we can engage with the complex relation between history and cultural memory, and as Hendel argues, consider these texts as a "palimpsest of past and present" (Hendel 2005: 45–47).

In this way, knowledge of, and interactions with a neighboring polity and people are cast in a deep time perspective (Hensel 2021a). As such, the association of Jacob and Esau with the polities of Israel/Judah and Edom is likely a later phenomenon in the development of the tradition, and unsurprisingly, ought not to be used to influence a history between them (Hendel 1987: 114–115; Crowell 2021: 177–264).[23] To illustrate, numerous characteristics of Esau stand contrary to other characteristics associated with Edom. Whereas Esau is depicted as lacking in intelligence, contrasted with the cunning of Jacob (Genesis 25, 27), other traditions associate Edom with wisdom (Jeremiah 49:7; Obadiah 1:8; Baruch 3:22–23; Job; Hendel 1987: 114–115). Similar, later emendations to the text may perhaps be seen in Isaac's proclamation of Esau/Edom's subservience to Jacob/Israel/Judah (Genesis 27:40), which contradicts the remainder of the narrative in which Jacob shows willing submission to Esau, and in the intimacy of their reunion (Genesis 32–33; Fleming 2012: 84; Crowell 2021: 224–228).

Despite being cast as a coarse and somewhat abrasive figure (Arnold 2009: 232–233), Esau is portrayed in sympathetic terms, a feature that further belies interpreting Esau as Jacob's enemy. Likewise, it is not Esau who engages in trickery and theft, but Jacob, creating something of a moral issue for later biblical commentaries (Krause 2008). Even with the humiliating events of Genesis 27, a simple contrast between Esau and the figure of Laban,

---

[23] Certain vignettes in the narrative, such as Esau's marriages, are contrasted with Jacob's in their exogenous nature (Genesis 36:2–5; 26:34 vs. Genesis 29–31; Arnold 2009: 308–311). These marriages (though inconsistent between these passages), serve to situate Esau and Edom with communities to the south and east, with the association with Ishmael's daughter evoking the social alliances between Edom and the Arab tribes in the context of trade.

representing Aram (Genesis 29–31), together with Esau's reacceptance of Jacob, places Esau in far higher regard (Fleming 2012: 83–85). In this fashion, an alternative way of looking at this text would be through the lens of the narrative "hero" (Jacob) and the uncultured "other" (Esau), a portrayal frequent in Near Eastern literature that emphasizes one figure as a literary foil to the other (Hendel 1987: 101–131; Hamori 2011: 633–636). The contrast between the two, with the later equation between Esau and Edom through various physical (red, hairy, hunter) and personality (coarse, abrasive, intellectually dim) characteristics, would serve to evoke in a Judahite audience a certain image of their eastern regional neighbor (Arnold 2009: 232–233).

These associations may be described as a pattern of "othering," defined as the "process which serves to mark and name those thought to be different from onself" – a key feature of identity formation processes (Weis 1995: 18). Consequently, these contrasts of the physical and intellectual characteristics of Jacob and Esau would serve to reify belongingness to communities who identified as Jacob's descendants in contrast with those associated with the figure of Esau, who at least in the surviving version of the narrative stand as metaphors for Israel/Judah and Edom. In all, the narratives portray a highly entangled relationship between Jacob/Judah/Israel and Esau/Edom, one of competition and conflict, but also closeness and reconciliation, standing as a unique metaphor to exemplify the multifaceted pattern of cross-cultural interaction in the northeastern Negev (Tebes 2006b; Hensel 2021a; Danielson 2022).

5.2 Entangled and Forgotten Gods

In light of such complexities of cultural memory interwoven in layers of etiology, it is highly intriguing that the Hebrew Bible does not once mention Qos, the foremost deity of Edom. In fact, regarding any specific deities of Edom, the biblical text is silent.[24] The only possible intimations of the existence of the neighboring deity Qos are hidden as a theophoric element in the name *barqôs* (ברקוס), found amidst a list of Persian period returned exiles decades after the kingdom of Edom had faded from the Levantine political stage (Ezra 2:53; Nehemiah 7:55). This silence regarding Qos is all the more striking as numerous passages characterize neighboring peoples in relation to major deities worshipped in their regions. For example, in the curses in Jeremiah 48–49, the god Kemosh is identified with Moab, and immediately afterward, Milkom with

---

[24] The Chronicler makes a vague reference to capturing the "gods of the people of Seir," though no specific deity names are included (2 Chronicles 25:14), and the late context and agenda of the Chronicler must be considered (Bartlett 1989: 194–196).

Ammon. Yet, in the same chapter, amidst a lengthy and hostile curse against Edom, no gods are mentioned. The absence of Qos stands amidst the numerous narratives and references to Edom in the biblical text, as well as the extensive cross-cultural interaction identified in the northeastern Negev.

A simple lack of knowledge of Qos on the part of the biblical writers is an insufficient explanation (Bartlett 1989: 195), as the shrine at Horvat Qitmit with its focus on this deity was located among settlements and forts claimed and administered by Judah. In fact, even in the epistolary of the Judahite administrators, two references to Qos are made (Aharoni 1981: nos. 12, 26). These inscriptions are poorly preserved, and these references appear to be solely theophoric, but the fact remains that this god was known to the people of Judah, and is attested in the administrative writings of Judahite elites. Even if a very late date for the composition of the Hebrew Bible is presumed, the inscriptional finds from Persian and Hellenistic period Idumea only indicate that the popularity and prominence of Qos had grown. Therefore, the exclusion of Qos from the text appears to have been intentional.

To further complicate the picture, scholars have long-noted that in many of the oldest texts in the Hebrew Bible (Schniedewind 2013: 51–72), it is in fact Yahweh who is most closely associated with the region of Edom and the surrounding deserts. For example, Judges 5:4 states regarding Yahweh: "when you went out from Seir, when you marched from the region of Edom." Similarly, Deuteronomy 33:2, describes Yahweh as having "dawned from Seir" while also connecting him with the Sinai and Paran, other neighboring desert regions. Further, from the desert site of Kuntillet ʿAjrud in northeastern Sinai, inscriptions were excavated that mention a "Yahweh of Teman and his Asherah," identifying Yahweh with Teman (Ahituv et al. 2012: 95–98, 105), a location in the environs of Edom (Knauf 1992b). This affiliation echoes the likely archaic text of Habakkuk 3:3 that states "God came from Teman." Beyond associations with Jerusalem and locales to the north, these references, and particularly the Kuntillet ʿAjrud inscriptions, indicate that traditions of Yahweh, or at least certain manifestations of Yahweh, were understood as relating to desert locales to the south and east of Judah.[25]

---

[25] There is yet debate surrounding the geographic and contextual origins of Yahweh, including the Midianite-Kenite hypothesis that is associated with Yahweh's desert origins (van Oorschot and Witte 2017; Lewis 2020; Fleming 2021; Miller 2021). Further, some scholars have argued for an Arabic linguistic etymology for Yahweh, based on the Arabic root *hwy* rather than the West Semitic *hwh* (Knauf 1988: 43–48; van der Toorn 1999); doing so would provide meanings for the name Yahweh such as "he who causes rain/lightening/enemies] to fall" or " . . . [wind] to blow," associating Yahweh with the characteristics of a storm god. However, see also discussion in Lewis (2020: 213–223) and Miller (2021: 16–18).

Outside of the biblical text, there are numerous inscriptional references that link Qos to the landscape of Edom and the surrounding deserts (Bartlett 1989; Dearman 1995; Knauf 1999; Kelley 2009; Danielson 2020b). While there is little direct iconographic evidence to reveal the nature of Qos, on the basis of associated imagery at sites such as Horvat Qitmit, Qos appears to have functioned as a type of Iron Age weather deity and/or divine warrior (Bartlett 1989: 200–204; Beck 1995: 187–190, 1996: 107–109; Dearman 1995; Knauf 1999: 377; Kelley 2009: 260–261; Danielson 2020b: 115–116). Etymologically, the name Qos (קוֹס) appears to be synonymous to the Arabic term for bow – *qaws* (قوس) – perhaps sharing an earlier proto-Semitic root, with the West Semitic derivation of bow as *qšt* (קֶשֶׁת; Knauf 1999: 676).[26] This meaning of "bow" in association with Qos, has been interpreted as further substantiating the idea of Qos as a weather deity/divine warrior, who are frequently depicted with bows.

Combined with the potential origins of Yahweh in Edom, the conspicuous omission of Qos from the biblical text has led some scholars to propose the silence to be an inadvertent admission of a shared religious past between Judah and Edom. In such interpretations, Yahweh and Qos are suggested to have been derived from an earlier El deity, with the resulting differences understood as alternate understandings promoted by different communities (Dearman 1995: 126–127). Alternative theories have Qos functioning as an epithet of Yahweh (Amzallag 2009: 392; Kelley 2009: 265), or even as the divinized bow (קֶשֶׁת) of Yahweh (Kelley 2009: 266; Habakkuk 3:9; Psalm 7:12–13; Genesis 9:13–16).

While this relationship and questions of origins remain unclear, with the dataset heavily biased toward a Yahwistic perspective, the entangled relations between these peoples and their gods exemplify the multifaceted, fraternal, and competitive nature of the biblical text's allusions to, and etiologies associated with this region. Whatever the motives the biblical writers had toward silencing Qos, the archaeology of Edom and the Negev has placed Qos in the center of the stage, necessitating more nuanced interpretations of the religious heritage of the northeastern Negev.

6 Edom in Judah: Social Entanglement in the Northeastern Negev

The northeastern Negev during the late Iron Age was a dynamic zone of cross-cultural interactions, economic enterprise, political and administrative investment, and imperial interest. The economic foundation of the region was centered on agropastoral subsistence, though during the late Iron Age, surplus grain production, an investment in wool and textiles, and a branch of the South Arabian trade

---

[26] Note that Qos is always written with a *sāmek* (ס) and never a *šîn/śîn* (שׁ).

amplified its economic output. This situation created a rich context for mobility, migration, and alliance-making among the diverse groups operating here, particularly between the persons and communities affiliated with the kingdoms of Judah and Edom. These complex interactions in the northeastern Negev are attested as early as the eighth century BCE, lasting until the early sixth century BCE, though they appear as but one chapter in a long-standing pattern of east-west movement and interaction across this region through the millennia (Erickson-Gini and Israel 2013; Ben-Dor Evian 2017; Finkelstein et al. 2018; Danielson 2023). Focusing on the late Iron Age and using socially sensitive material culture proxies for aspects of identity, this work has engaged with culinary traditions, religious practices, dialects and naming conventions, and rich textual traditions in order to explore and describe the multifaceted social entanglements that characterized the region.

First, from the material culture record, culinary ceramics reveal a diverse range of traditions that can be traced spatially, diachronically, and socially. Whereas the military forts of the region such as Horvat Tov and Tel Arad appear to have maintained a rather homogenous set of traditions, other forts including Horvat ʿUza and the settlements of Tel Malhata and Tel ʿAroer reveal a diversity of culinary practices integrated into the very fabric of the sites themselves – even in a single house. This entanglement of culinary traditions is best exemplified at sites located along the major east-west road through the Beersheba-Arad Valley, reflecting movements from the Mediterranean Coastal Plain to the west, and southern Jordan to the southeast. The preponderance of cooking vessels in the northeastern Negev that are similar to those most popular in Edom attest to the frequency of interaction between these regions, and migration westward from Edom. This movement is interpreted as the result of transhumance, and various forms of social alliances in the context of trade, as well as the taking of prisoners and the practice of enslaving people. Further, distributions of elaborately decorated tableware and its association with contexts of feasting reveal the unique places where alliances were created, many of which are evident at key nodes of the transregional trade network.

With regard to religious practices, while the traditions of Edom and Judah have frequently been cast as highly divergent, these differences only become starkly apparent when one examines broader regional and state-sanctioned activity. At the domestic level, household and family practices appear to have been remarkably similar, regardless of which deity they were oriented toward. This situation ought not to be surprising. After all, deities inhabit and are at home in specific regions, and one's orientation toward that deity could well shift depending on one's geographic location. Yet, even in the northeastern Negev, Qos must be viewed as a local deity, at home in the large sanctuary at Horvat Qitmit. The fact that Horvat Qitmit remained in use and undisturbed for close to a century, signals the acceptance of Qos' belonging by the majority of the population, many of whom appear to have been more closely aligned with the deity Yahweh.

Similarly, a limited, but intriguing corpus of inscriptions allows for preliminary interpretations concerning the dialects spoken in these regions. The inhabitants of southern Judah and Edom spoke a mutually intelligible language, though one marked by identifiable differences. These differences would have been noticeable in pronunciations, phonological stresses, and especially in standardized greetings and blessings. Thus, differences were a characteristic feature of the region, with alternative pronunciations and deities invoked in greetings and blessings formalized in written letters, which similarly bear the markings of divergent scribal traditions associated with the separate administrations of Judah and Edom.

This complex history of mobility, interaction, and kinship is referenced in biblical traditions that mythologize this region and its inhabitants as the descendants of the patriarchal figures, Jacob and Esau. The legends surrounding these twin brothers highlight competition, but also reconciliation and acceptance. The competition and shared heritage between the figures of Jacob and Esau as reflected in the Hebrew Bible, likewise appear to echo the complex and poorly understood origins of Yahweh and Qos, two gods with close relations to the arid regions of the Negev and Edom, and perhaps even to one another.

Therefore, in contrast to secondary scholarship that tends to essentialize Judah and Edom as internally homogeneous cultural totalities that were distinct from one another, the extensive archaeological, inscriptional, and textual evidence reveals a world of porous boundaries and dynamic, multifaceted entanglement. It was only after the region's destruction that this multicultural legacy was simplified and reworked.

7 Epilogue: Destruction and Defamation

The settlement system in the northeastern Negev met a destructive end sometime in the early part of the sixth century BCE. Major destructions have been noted at all of the settlements and forts in the region. In fact, the only site to not bear evidence of this destruction is Horvat Qitmit, which nonetheless was contemporaneously abandonned. By all accounts, these destructions and abandonments appear to have been largely contemporary, evidencing a complete collapse of the regional settlement system in a short period of time. These sites remained uninhabited for more than a century until a limited reoccupation at several sites began. On its own, the archaeological data, namely pottery, suggests a late seventh or more likely early sixth century BCE date for the destructions and abandonments. Such dating builds on the extensive comparative assemblages and destructions in the region to the north, where the agent of destruction is understood to be the Neo-Babylonian empire under Nebuchadnezzar II.

Following suit, many of the destructions at the Negev sites have been interpreted as the result of these Babylonian campaigns, perhaps in 598 BCE, or more likely, in relation to the destructive events surrounding Zedekiah's revolt and the Babylonian destruction of Jerusalem and Judah in 586 BCE (Lipschits 2005: 224–229). Judah well-evidences the severity of these campaigns and does not recover for centuries (Faust 2012). Other major interpretations of the destruction of the settlement system have centered on Edom where it is seen as either an agent of Babylon or as acting on its own accord, initiated by the ruling elite or by culturally affiliated groups of "Edomite" nomads.

Interpretations of Edom as an aggressor in the northeastern Negev against Judah have been driven in part by biblical polemics against Edom that reference a hostile role played by Edom during the Babylonian invasions. These are especially prevalent in the prophetic texts (e.g., Isaiah 34, 63:1–6, Jeremiah 49:7–22; Ezekiel 35:1, 36:15, Joel 4:19–21, Amos 1:9–12, Obadiah, Malachi 1:1–5; see also Psalm 137, Lamentations 4:21–22; Assis 2006, 2016: 74–162; Ben Zvi 2022; Edelman 2022). The language used in these texts stands in stark contrast to the fraternal language used elsewhere in the Hebrew Bible, as discussed in Section 5. For example, the text of Isaiah reads:

> When my sword has drunk its fill in the heavens, upon Edom it will fall, upon the people I have doomed to judgment. Yahweh has a sword; it is sated with blood; it is gorged with fat, with the blood of lambs and goats, with the fat of the kidneys of rams. For Yahweh has a sacrifice in Bozrah [Busayra], a great slaughter in the land of Edom (Isaiah 34:5–6).

The text highlights a deep desire to see violence cast on Edom, couched in the language of a proclamation from Judah's god, Yahweh. Similarly, the text of Jeremiah reads:

> For by myself I have sworn, says Yahweh, that Bozrah [Busayra] shall become an object of horror and ridicule, a waste, and an object of cursing, and all her towns shall be perpetual wastes . . . Edom shall become an object of horror; everyone who passes by it will be horrified and will hiss because of all its disasters (Jeremiah 49:13, 17)

Indeed, the entirety of the book of Obadiah itself serves as a polemic against Edom, here with a direct equation made between Esau and Edom, and Judah and Jacob, in a starkly different tone than the patriarchal narratives previously described. The reasoning provided for this hostility against Edom is argued to be present in texts such as Psalm 137:7: "Remember, [Yahweh], against the Edomites, the day of Jerusalem's fall, how they said, 'Tear it down! Tear it down! Down to its foundations!'" Here, Psalm 137 seeks to identify Edom as a direct aggressor in the fall of Jerusalem during the Babylonian invasions. These texts formed a large part of the zeitgeist concerning Edom during early exploration and excavation in the Negev.

The perspectives of a hostile Edom were largely reinforced during the excavation and publication of a series of ostraca from the Judahite fort at Tel Arad. In the inscriptions, a number of references are made to Edom/Edomites and to Qos-named persons, but several ostraca stand out. First, Ostracon No. 40 alludes to correspondence from Edom, prior to ending with the line: "The King of Judah should know [that w]e cannot send the [. . . and th]is is the evil that Edo[m has done]" (Aharoni 1981: 70–74). Next, on the preserved latter half of Ostracon No. 24, the inscription appears to describe troop movements, namely fifty men from Arad, and an undetermined amount from Qinah (Horvat ʿUza?) to be transferred to Ramat Negeb (Tel ʿIra?), "lest anything happen to the city." The inscription ends with the ominous-sounding note: "I have sent to warn you today: [Get] the men to Elishaʿ: Lest Edom should come there" (Aharoni 1981: 46–49). These two ostraca with their allusions to "evil" done by Edom, and troop movement, apparently borne out of concern for the "arrival" of Edom, together supported the notion of Edom's hostility, and on the basis of their association with the final stratum of the fort prior to its destruction,[27] were taken as evidence of the culpability of Edom (Beit-Arieh 1995a: 311–316, 1996).

The fact that the major settlements in Edom were not destroyed at this time (rather several decades later), along with the excavation of much "Edomite" material culture in the Negev in the decades following the publication of the Arad Ostraca, appeared to support a picture of an invading Edom as the cause of these destructions. Yet as has long been noted, and as this analysis has demonstrated, there are numerous challenges with this interpretation (Finkelstein 1992, 1995: 139–144; Singer-Avitz 1999: 8–10). Rather, as has been discussed previously, the "Edomite" material culture is not found superimposed over the destruction debris but rather is present for the entire century-and-a-half preceding this destruction, integrated into the social fabric of these settlements (Tebes 2006a, 2007a; Thareani 2010, 2014; Danielson 2021, 2022). Thus, it was the mixed and entangled Judahite-Edomite community that was destroyed, with no evidence of a new occupation atop the ruins.

---

[27] Ostracon No. 40 was originally dated to Stratum VIII (Aharoni 1981: 74, n.1), though subsequent analysis has convincingly argued for it to be reassigned to Stratum VI, the final stratum at Arad prior to its destruction in the early sixth century BCE (Naʾaman 2003).

Furthermore, the Arad Ostraca are not entirely unambiguous, and alternative interpretations have been proposed. For example, Philippe Guillaume has argued for an alternative translation that shifts the ideas of "evil" and "invasion" toward conflicts surrounding grazing rights (2013). Guillaume's hypothesis serves well to emphasize that present-day events and borders may be playing an outsized role in interpreting the nature of interactions in this region. Even in the biblical text, where it might initially appear somewhat straightforward that Edom was involved in the destruction of Jerusalem, the situation is far from clear. Notably, the majority of polemics against Edom feature most prominently in later, exilic and postexilic literature. From the texts that most closely describe the immediate events surrounding the Babylonian invasion, the picture is quite different. When describing the events surrounding the arrival of Babylon, for example, passages in Kings allude to local agents operating as proxies of the Babylonians in raids against Judah (i.e., Arameans, Ammonites, and Moabites; 2 Kings 24:2). However, among the numerous neighbors listed as aggressors against Judah, Edom is not present. In other instances, however, Edom is mentioned as a region of refuge for Judahites fleeing the Babylonian conquest (Jeremiah 40:11; Ben Zvi 2022: 325–327).

The fact that Edom survived relatively unscathed during the initial Babylonian invasions has been suggested as indicative of Edom benefitting from the demise of Judah, as though their fortunes were part of a zero-sum game. Elie Assis, for example, holds that "Edom and Judah were rival and neighboring peoples and they were in constant conflict" (2006: 11). However, more recent analyses of the Negev and Edom have emphasized cooperation between the regions in the larger trade network (e.g., Danielson 2023). The fortunes of one were tied to the other, and the demise of the northeastern Negev settlement system would have had dire consequences on the viability of the continued trade from which they both profited (Danielson 2023: 158–162). In other words, the destruction of the northeastern Negev does not appear to have been in the best interest of Edom as a political entity.

Alternative hypotheses have suggested that the hostile-seeming "Edom" of the Arad letters could be describing seminomadic groups in the Negev who were culturally aligned with southern Jordan (Thareani 2014). This understanding highlights the Negev's diverse groups and the inegalitarian nature of relations between them. In this interpretation, it is not entirely the Babylonian armies who were responsible for the collapse of the region. While they may have destroyed key sites, their invasion and destruction of Jerusalem would have destabilized the region, presenting opportunities for aggrieved or opportunistic groups to raid or destroy other settlements. This interpretation further builds on the multiple geopolitical crises facing the southern Levant at the close of the seventh and in the early sixth centuries BCE: the withdrawal of Assyria, the political vacuum briefly filled by the twenty-sixth Dynasty Egyptians, and then the destructive nature of Babylonian rule toward the region (Schipper 2010; Fantalkin 2011; Thareani 2014: 201–203; Itkin 2020: 80–83). With the inability of the Assyrians, or Judah, to fully enforce stability in this region, Yifat Thareani asserts that local seminomadic groups took advantage of the situation, eventually working in collaboration with the Babylonian program (2014: 201–203). These destructions then were likely not part of a single event, but rather a series of unorganized destructions taking place over a short period of time (Thareani 2014: 201–203).

Recent analyses may similarly be identifying further support for this interpretation. Namely, archaeomagnetic analyses conducted at destroyed sites have presented the possibility of more precisely dating destruction levels (Vaknin et al. 2022). In relation to the northeastern Negev, this analysis has posited that Tel Malhata was likely only destroyed about a decade after the Babylonian destruction of Jerusalem in 586 BCE. This interpretation suggests that local southern Levantine agents were responsible, at least for the destruction of Malhata, hinting again at Edom as a potential culprit. This revised dating might even suggest that trade through the Negev continued for about a decade after the destruction of Jerusalem and Judah in 586 BCE, with Edom as the most likely beneficiary. This dating, however, is relatively new and in this context limited to Tel Malhata; thus, conclusions remain tentative.

While certain lines of evidence point to the likelihood of hostile actions during the sixth century BCE, there remains little firm and definitive archaeological evidence for the blame placed on Edom, and more than sufficient data to unequivocally demonstrate the entangled nature of social interactions between Judah and Edom. In fact, the century and a half of close productive relations between the two regions ought to serve as a strong counterpoint to any interpretation that prioritizes violence and hostility as the defining characteristic of interactions in this region. The question yet remains, however, of the hostility, hurt, and anger directed at Edom in the biblical text surrounding the memory of the destruction of Jerusalem. Some of the Judahite blame is suggested to have been prejudice against a former neighbor who, from the perspective of a devastated Judah, survived the Babylonian campaigns unscathed, and stood to profit from Judah's demise (Bartlett 1989: 155–156), in essence becoming a scapegoat in late prophetic and poetic texts (Assis 2006; Tebes 2011a: 241–245).

Further developing this idea, Juan Tebes suggests that the blame laid on Edom in this literature is more a reflection of a later Judean perception of Edomite participation, which eventually for them, came to be a reality (Tebes 2011a: 232). During the late Persian period (fourth century BCE), this region of the northeastern Negev came to be known as "Idumea," bearing a memory of the name of late Iron Age Edom. Numerous ostraca from the region also record its inhabitants as Qos-named persons, appearing to thus preserve certain cultural elements of the late Iron Age (Hensel et al. 2022). Returning Judean exiles, upon witnessing a greater social transformation of this formerly "Judahite" region with the numerous legacies of Edom present, may have expressed their distaste in the biblical texts that were codified at this time (Tebes 2011a: 248–252).

Other studies have argued that treaty betrayal was at the origin of the anti-Edomite sentiment. According to this perspective, geographic proximity as well as mutual economic interests strongly indicate that periods of cooperation would have been accompanied by the formation of treaties between Judah and Edom, and that evidence of these treaties may be found in the kinship language that is often applied to Edom in the biblical text (Dykehouse 2008, 2013). Consequently, as covenants and treaties were codified through the language of kinship and responsibility, during the Babylonian crisis, a failure of Edom to lend aid to Judah would have been perceived not only as a rejection of Judahite/Israelite kinship, but instead a creation of kinship between Edom and Babylon (Dykehouse 2008: 292). Further, from the perspective of the postexilic Judeans, the rejection of kinship would have been accompanied by the Idumean "inheritance" of lands that Yahweh had formerly allocated to Israel/Judah (Anderson 2011: 5; Crowell 2021: 383).

Edom met its own end in the middle of the sixth century BCE. An inscription of Nabonidus from the site of Selaʿ, a short distance north of Busayra, presents the most likely candidate for the destructions at key symbolic areas at Busayra at this time (Bienkowski 2002a: 475–478; Crowell 2007; Da Riva 2020). Nabonidus' inscription appears related to his broader enterprise in North Arabia, referenced in Babylonian sources (Beaulieu 1989: 218–232), and corroborated by inscriptions from North Arabia (Eichmann et al. 2006; Hausleiter and Schaudig 2016). Nabonidus' Arabian campaign appears centered around a broader program to more fully orient the Arabian trade routes toward Babylonia and away from the southern Levant (Danielson 2023: 151–153, 159–163). This program coincides with a major decline in Edom, with numerous site abandonments, destructions, and a shift toward non-sedentary modes of subsistence and migrations to surrounding regions. One such destination lay in what remained of Judah, in the Shephelah and southern Judean Highlands adjacent to the yet-ruined Negev, a region that would later become known as Idumea (Hensel et al. 2022). This movement would have followed the late Iron Age route, echoing the connections that had so well defined the interactions between the peoples of Edom and Judah.

References

Ababsa, M., ed. (2013). *Atlas of Jordan: History, Territories and Society*, Beirut: Institut Français du Proche-Orient.

Agnew, J. (1994). The Territorial Trap: The Geographical Assumptions of International Relations Theory. *Review of International Political Economy*, **1**, 53–80.

Aharoni, Y. (1981). *Arad Inscriptions*, Jerusalem: Israel Exploration Society.

Ahituv, S. (2008). *Echoes from the Past: Hebrew and Cognate Inscriptions from the Biblical Period*, Jerusalem: Carta.

Ahituv, S., Eshel, E., & Meshel, Z. (2012). The Inscriptions. In Z. Meshel, ed., *Kuntillet ʿAjrud (Horvat Teman): An Iron Age II Religious Site on the Judah-Sinai Border*. Jerusalem: Israel Exploration Society, pp. 73–142.

Albertz, R., Nakhai, B. A., Olyan, S., & Schmitt, R., eds. (2014). *Family and Household Religion: Toward a Synthesis of Old Testament Studies, Archaeology, Epigraphy, and Cultural Studies*, Winona Lake, IN: Eisenbrauns.

Albertz, R., & Schmitt, R. (2012). *Family and Household Religion in Ancient Israel and the Levant*, Winona Lake, IN: Eisenbrauns.

Aldrin, E. (2016). Names and Identity. In C. Hough, ed., *The Oxford Handbook of Names and Naming*. Oxford: Oxford University Press, pp. 382–94.

Altmann, P., & Fu, J., eds. (2014). *Feasting in the Archaeology and Texts of the Bible and the Ancient Near East*, Winona Lake, IN: Eisenbrauns.

Amzallag, N. (2009). Yahweh, the Canaanite God of Metallurgy? *Journal for the Study of the Old Testament*, **33**(4), 387–404.

Anderson, B. (2011). *Brotherhood and Inheritance: A Canonical Reading of the Esau and Edom Traditions*, New York: T&T Clark.

Appadurai, A. (1981). Gastro-Politics in Hindu South Asia. *American Ethnologist*, **8**(3), 494–511.

Arie, E., Rosen, B., & Namdar, D. (2020). Cannabis and Frankincense at the Judahite Shrine of Arad. *Tel Aviv*, **47**, 5–28.

Arnold, B. (2009). *Genesis*, Cambridge: Cambridge University Press.

Assis, E. (2006). Why Edom? On the Hostility towards Jacob's Brother in Prophetic Sources. *Vetus Testamentum*, **56**(1), 1–20.

Assis, E. (2016). *Identity in Conflict: The Struggle Between Esau and Jacob, Edom and Israel*, Winona Lake, IN: Eisenbrauns.

Bartlett, J. (1989). *Edom and the Edomites*, Sheffield: Journal for the Study of the Old Testament.

Bartlett, J. (1992). Edom. In D. N. Freedman, ed., *The Anchor Bible Dictionary Vol. 2*. New York: Doubleday, pp. 287–301.

Bartlett, J. (1995). Edom in the Nonprophetical Corpus. In D. Edelman, ed., *You Shall Not Abhor an Edomite for He Is Your Brother: Edom and Seir in History and Tradition*. Atlanta, GA: Scholars Press, pp. 13–21.

Bartlett, J. (1999). Edomites and Idumaeans. *Palestine Exploration Quarterly*, **131**(2), 102–14.

Beaulieu, P.-A. (1989). *The Reign of Nabonidus King of Babylon 556–539 B.C.*, New Haven, CT: Yale University Press.

Beck, P. (1995). Catalogue of Cult Objects and Study of the Iconography. In I. Beit-Arieh, ed., *Horvat Qitmit: An Edomite Shrine in the Biblical Negev*. Tel Aviv: Institute of Archaeology, Tel Aviv University, pp. 27–197.

Beck, P. (1996). Horvat Qitmit Revisited via ʿEn Hazeva. *Tel Aviv*, **23**, 102–14.

Beck, P. (1999). Human Figurine with a Tambourine. In I. Beit-Arieh, ed., *Tel ʿIra: A Stronghold in the Biblical Negev*. Tel Aviv: Institute of Archaeology, Tel Aviv University, pp. 386–94.

Beit-Arieh, I. (1995a). *Horvat Qitmit: An Edomite Shrine in the Biblical Negev*, Tel Aviv: Institute of Archaeology, Tel Aviv University.

Beit-Arieh, I. (1995b). Inscriptions. In I. Beit-Arieh, ed., *Horvat Qitmit: An Edomite Shrine in the Biblical Negev*. Tel Aviv: Institute of Archaeology, Tel Aviv University, pp. 258–68.

Beit-Arieh, I. (1995c). The Edomites in Cisjordan. In D. Edelman, ed., *You Shall Not Abhor an Edomite for He Is Your Brother: Edom and Seir in History and Tradition*. Atlanta: Scholars Press, pp. 33–40.

Beit-Arieh, I. (1996). Edomites Advance into Judah — Israelite Defensive Fortresses Inadequate. *Biblical Archaeology Review*, **22**(6), 28–36.

Beit-Arieh, I. (2007a). Epigraphic Finds. In I. Beit-Arieh, ed., *Horvat ʿUza and Horvat Radum: Two Fortresses in the Biblical Negev*. Tel Aviv: Institute of Archaeology, Tel Aviv University, pp. 122–87.

Beit-Arieh, I. (2007b). *Horvat ʿUza and Horvat Radum: Two Fortresses in the Biblical Negev*, Tel Aviv: Institute of Archaeology, Tel Aviv University.

Beit-Arieh, I. (2015). A Phallus-Shaped Clay Object. In I. Beit-Arieh & L. Freud, eds., *Tel Malhata: A Central City in the Biblical Negev*. Winona Lake, IN: Eisenbrauns, p. 580.

Beit-Arieh, I., & Freud, L. (2015). Iron Age IIC: Northeastern Negev. In S. Gitin, ed., *The Ancient Pottery of Israel and its Neighbors: From the Iron Age through the Hellenistic Period*. Jerusalem: Israel Exploration Society, pp. 365–82.

Beit-Arieh, I., Freud, L., & Tal, O. (2015). Summary. In I. Beit-Arieh & L. Freud, eds., *Tel Malhata: A Central City in the Biblical Negev*. Winona Lake, IN: Eisenbrauns, pp. 739–44.

van Bekkum, K. (2023). Competing Chronologies, Competing Histories: Ancient Israel and the Chronology of the Southern Levant ca. 1200–587 BCE. In K. Keimer and G. Pierce, eds., *The Ancient Israelite World*. New York: Routledge, pp. 34–53.

Ben Zvi, E. (2022). Edom as a Complex Site of Memory among the Literati of Late Persian/Early Hellenistic Judah: Some Observations. In B. Hensel, E. Ben Zvi, & D. Edelman, eds., *About Edom and Idumea in the Persian Period: Recent Research and Approaches from Archaeology, Hebrew Bible Studies and Ancient Near Eastern Studies*. Sheffield: Equinox, pp. 321–37.

Ben-Dor Evian, S. (2017). Follow the Negebite Ware Road. In O. Lipschits, Y. Gadot, & M. Adams, eds., *Rethinking Israel: Studies in the History and Archaeology of Ancient Israel in Honor of Israel Finkelstein*. Winona Lake, IN: Eisenbrauns, pp. 19–28.

Bennett, C. (1982). Neo-Assyrian Influence in Transjordan. *Studies in the History and Archaeology of Jordan*, **1**, 181–7.

Bennett, C., & Bienkowski, P. (1995). *Excavations at Tawilan in Southern Jordan*, Oxford: Oxford University Press.

Ben-Shlomo, D. (2014). Tell Jemmeh, Philistia and the Neo-Assyrian Empire during the Late Iron Age. *Levant*, **46**(1), 58–88.

Ben-Shlomo, D., Bouzaglou, L., Mommsen, H., & Sterba, J. (2023). Production Centers of Cooking Pots in Iron Age Judah. *Archaeometry*, **65**(1), 84–104.

Ben-Shlomo, D., Shai, I., Zukerman, A., & Maeir, A. (2008). Cooking Identities: Aegean-Style Cooking Jugs and Cultural Interaction in Iron Age Philistia and Neighboring Regions. *American Journal of Archaeology*, **112**, 225–46.

Ben-Yehoshua, S., Borowitz, C., & Hanuš, L. (2012). Frankincense, Myrrh, and Balm of Gilead: Ancient Spices of Southern Arabia and Judea. *Horticultural Reviews*, **39**, 1–76.

Ben-Yosef, E. (2019). The Architectural Bias in Current Biblical Archaeology. *Vetus Testamentum*, **69**, 361–87.

Ben-Yosef, E. (2021). Rethinking the Social Complexity of Early Iron Age Nomads. *Jerusalem Journal of Archaeology*, **1**, 155–79.

Ben-Yosef, E., Liss, B., Yagel, O., et al. (2019). Ancient Technology and Punctuated Change: Detecting the Emergence of the Edomite Kingdom in the Southern Levant. *PLOS ONE*, **14**(9), 1–16.

Ben-Yosef, E., Najjar, M., & Levy, T. (2014). Local Iron Age Trade Routes in Northern Edom: From the Faynan Copper Ore District to the Highlands. In T. Levy, M. Najjar, & E. Ben-Yosef, eds., *New Insights into the Iron Age Archaeology of Edom, Southern Jordan*. Los Angeles: Cotsen Institute of Archaeology, pp. 493–576.

Bienkowski, P. (2002a). *Busayra: Excavations by Crystal-M. Bennett 1971–1980*, Oxford: Oxford University Press.

Bienkowski, P. (2002b). The Pottery. In P. Bienkowski, ed., *Busayra: Excavations by Crystal-M. Bennett 1971–1980*. Oxford: Oxford University Press, pp. 233–352.

Bienkowski, P. (2011). *Umm al-Biyara: Excavations by Crystal-M. Bennett in Petra 1960–1965*, Oxford: Oxbow Books.

Bienkowski, P. (2015). Iron Age IIC: Transjordan. In S. Gitin, ed., *The Ancient Pottery of Israel and its Neighbors: From the Iron Age through the Hellenistic Period*. Jerusalem: Israel Exploration Society, pp. 419–34.

Bienkowski, P. (2022). The Formation of Edom: An Archaeological Critique of the "Early Edom" Hypothesis. *Bulletin of ASOR*, **388**, 113–32.

Bloch-Smith, E. (2002). Solomon's Temple: The Politics of Ritual Space. In B. Gittlen, ed., *Sacred Time Sacred Place: Archaeology and the Religion of Israel*. Winona Lake, IN: Eisenbrauns, pp. 83–94.

Blum, E. (2012). The Jacob Tradition. In C. Evans, J. Lohr, & D. Petersen, eds., *The Book of Genesis: Composition, Perception, and Interpretation*. Leiden: Brill, pp. 181–211.

Bodel, J., & Olyan, S., eds. (2008). *Household and Family Religion in Antiquity*, Malden, MA: Blackwell.

Bouzaglou, L., & Ben-Shlomo, D. (2023). A "chaîne opératoire" Perspective on Iron Age II Judean Cooking Pots. Archaeological and Anthropological Sciences **15**(6): 1–32.

Bray, T., ed. (2003). *The Archaeology and Politics of Food and Feasting in Early States and Empires*, New York: Kluwer Academic.

Brighton, S. (2015). Immigrant Foodways. In K. Metheny & M. Beaudry, eds., *Archaeology of Food: An Encyclopedia*. New York: Rowman & Littlefield, pp. 262–64.

Bron, F., & Lemaire, A. (2009). Nouvelle inscription sabéenne et le commerce en Transeuphratène. *Transeuphratène*, **38**, 11–29.

Brown, S. (2018a). Dining under Assyrian Rule: Foodways in Iron Age Edom. In C. Tyson & V. Herrmann, eds., *Imperial Peripheries in the Neo-Assyrian Period*. Boulder, CO: University Press of Colorado, pp. 150–76.

Brown, S. (2018b). *Living on the Edge of Empire: Edomite Households in the First Millennium B.C.E.* (Unpublished Ph.D. Dissertation), University of California, Berkeley.

Brulotte, R., & Di Giovine, M., eds. (2014). *Edible Identities: Food as Cultural Heritage*, Surrey: Ashgate.

Byrne, R. (2003). Early Assyrian Contacts with Arabs and the Impact on Levantine Vassal Tribute. *Bulletin of the American Schools of Oriental Research*, **331**, 11–25.

Cavigneaux, A., & Ismail, B. (1990). Die Statthalter von Suḫu und Mari im 8. Jh. v. Chr. *Baghdader Mitteilungen*, **21**, 321–456.

Cohen, R., & Bernick-Greenberg, H. (2007). *Excavations at Kadesh Barnea (Tell el-Qudeirat) 1976–1982*, Jerusalem: Israel Antiquities Authority.

Cohen, R., & Yisrael, Y. (1995). The Iron Age Fortresses at ʿEn Ḥaṣeva. *The Biblical Archaeologist*, **58**(4), 223–35.

Cohen, R., & Yisrael, Y. (1996). Smashing the Idols: Piecing Together an Edomite Shrine in Judah. *Biblical Archaeology Review*, **22**(4), 40–51.

Cohen-Sasson, E., Varoner, O., Frieman, E., & Herriott, C. (2021). Gorer Tower and the Biblical Edom Road. *Palestine Exploration Quarterly*, **153**(2), 113–28.

Colvin, S. (2010). Greek Dialects in the Archaic and Classical Ages. In E. Bakker, ed., *A Companion to the Ancient Greek Language*. Malden, MA: Wiley Blackwell, pp. 200–12.

Cordova, C. (2007). *Millennial Landscape Change in Jordan: Geoarchaeology and Cultural Ecology*, Tucson, AZ: University of Arizona Press.

Crowell, B. (2007). Nabonidus, as-Silaʿ, and the Beginning of the End of Edom. *Bulletin of the American Schools of Oriental Research*, **348**, 75–88.

Crowell, B. (2021). *Edom at the Edge of Empire: A Social and Political History*, Atlanta, GA: Society of Biblical Literature.

Da Riva, R. (2020). The Nabonidus Inscription in Sela (Jordan): Epigraphic Study and Historical Meaning. *Zeitschrift für Assyriologie und vorderasiatische Archäologie*, **110**(2), 176–95.

Dalley, S. (2017). Assyrian Warfare. In E. Frahm, ed., *A Companion to Assyria*. Malden, MA: Wiley Blackwell, pp. 522–33.

Damm, J. (2022). Identity at the Twilight of Empire: Domestic Foodways and Cultural Practice at 12th Century BC Beth-Shean. In L. Battini, A. Brody, & S. Steadman, eds., *No Place Like Home: Ancient Near Eastern Houses and Households*. Oxford: Archaeopress, pp. 92–110.

Danielson, A. (2020a). *Edom in Judah: An Archaeological Investigation of Identity, Interaction, and Social Entanglement in the Negev During the*

Late Iron Age (8th–6th Centuries BCE) (Unpublished Ph.D. Dissertation), University of California, Los Angeles.

Danielson, A. (2020b). On the History and Evolution of QWS: The Portrait of a First Millennium BCE Deity Explored through Community Identity. *Journal of Ancient Near Eastern Religions*, **20**, 113–89.

Danielson, A. (2021). Culinary Traditions in the Borderlands of Judah and Edom in the Late Iron Age. *Tel Aviv*, **48**, 87–111.

Danielson, A. (2022). Edom in Judah: Identity and Social Entanglement in the Late Iron Age Negev. In B. Hensel, E. Ben Zvi, & D. Edelman, eds., *About Edom and Idumea in the Persian Period: Recent Research and Approaches from Archaeology, Hebrew Bible Studies and Ancient Near East Studies*. Sheffield: Equinox, pp. 117–50.

Danielson, A. (2023). Trade, Kingdom, and Empire: Edom and the South Arabian Trade. *Journal of Ancient Near Eastern History*, **10**, 139–75.

Danielson, A., Arbuckle MacLeod, C., Hamm, M. J. et al. (2022). Testing and Disrupting Ontologies: Using the Database of Religious History as a Pedagogical Tool. *Religions*, **13**(9), 793.

Danielson, A., & Fessler, H. (2023). Tall al-Khalayfi as a Test Case for Assyrian-Levantine Collaboration. *Israel Exploration Journal*, **73**(1), 34–55.

Darby, E. (2014). *Interpreting Judean Pillar Figurines: Gender and Empire in Judean Apotropaic Ritual*, Tübingen: Mohr Siebeck.

Daviau, P. M. M. (2001). Family Religion: Evidence for the Paraphernalia of the Domestic Cult. In P. M. M. Daviau, J. W. Wevers, & M. Weigl, eds., *The World of the Arameans II: Studies in History and Archaeology in Honour of Paul-Eugene Dion*. Sheffield, pp. 199–229.

Daviau, P. M. M. (2012). Diversity in the Cultic Setting: Temples and Shrines in Central Jordan and the Negev. In J. Kamlah, ed., *Temple Building and Temple Cult: Architecture and Cultic Paraphernalia of Temples in the Levant (2.– 1. Mill. B.C.E.)*. Wiesbaden: Harrassowitz Verlag, pp. 435–58.

Dearman, A. (1995). Edomite Religion: A Survey and an Examination of Some Recent Contributions. In D. Edelman, ed., *You Shall Not Abhor an Edomite for He Is Your Brother: Edom and Seir in History and Tradition*. Atlanta: Scholars Press, pp. 119–36.

Dever, W. (2014). The Judean "Pillar-Base Figurines:" Mothers or "Mother-Goddesses"? In R. Albertz, B. A. Nakhai, S. Olyan, & R. Schmitt, eds., *Family and Household Religion: Toward a Synthesis of Old Testament Studies, Archaeology, Epigraphy, and Cultural Studies*. Winona Lake, IN: Eisenbrauns, pp. 129–42.

Diaz-Andreu, M., Lucy, S., Babić, S., & Edwards, D., eds. (2005). *The Archaeology of Identity: Approaches to Gender, Age, Status, Ethnicity and Religion*, New York: Routledge.

Dietler, M. (2001). Theorizing the Feast: Rituals of Consumption, Commensal Politics, and Power in African Contexts. In M. Dietler & B. Hayden, eds., *Feasts: Archaeological and Ethnographic Perspectives on Food, Politics, and Power*. Washington D.C.: Smithsonian Institution Press, pp. 65–114.

Dietler, M., & Herbich, I. (1998). Habitus, Techniques, Style: An Integrated Approach to the Social Understanding of Material Culture and Boundaries. In M. Stark, ed., *The Archaeology of Social Boundaries*. Washington, D. C.: Smithsonian Institution Press, pp. 232–63.

Divito, R. (1993). The Tell el-Kheleifeh Inscriptions. In G. Pratico, ed., *Nelson Glueck's 1938–1940 Excavations at Tell el-Kheleifeh: A Reappraisal*. Atlanta, GA: Scholars Press, pp. 51–63.

Dykehouse, J. C. (2008). *An Historical Reconstruction of Edomite Treaty Betrayal in the Sixth Century B.C.E. Based on Biblical, Epigraphic, and Archaeological Data* (Unpublished Ph.D. Dissertation), Baylor University.

Dykehouse, J. C. (2013). Biblical Evidence from Obadiah and Psalm 137 for an Edomite Treaty Betrayal of Judah in the Sixth Century B.C.E. *Antiguo Oriente*, **11**, 75–128.

Ebeling, J. (2010). *Women's Lives in Biblical Times*, New York: T&T Clark.

Edelman, D. (1995). Edom: A Historical Geography. In D. Edelman, ed., *You Shall Not Abhor an Edomite for He Is Your Brother: Edom and Seir in History and Tradition*. Atlanta, GA: Scholars Press, pp. 1–12.

Edelman, D. (2022). Late Historical Edom and Reading Edom, Seir and Esau in the Prophetic Literature through Persian Lenses: Preliminary Observations. In B. Hensel, E. Ben Zvi, & D. Edelman, eds., *About Edom and Idumea in the Persian Period: Recent Research and Approaches from Archaeology, Hebrew Bible Studies, and Ancient Near Eastern Studies*. Sheffield: Equinox, pp. 392–428.

Edwards, D. (2005). The Archaeology of Religion. In M. Díaz-Andreu, S. Lucy, S. Babić, & D. Edwards, eds., *The Archaeology of Identity: Approaches to Gender, Age, Status, Ethnicity and Religion*. New York: Routledge, pp. 110–28.

Eichmann, R., Schaudig, H., & Hausleiter, A. (2006). Archaeology and Epigraphy at Tayma (Saudi Arabia). *Arabian Archaeology and Epigraphy*, **17**, 163–76.

Eph'al, I. (1982). *The Ancient Arabs: Nomads on the Borders of the Fertile Crescent 9th–5th Centuries BC*, Leiden: E. J. Brill.

Erickson-Gini, T., & Israel, Y. (2013). Excavating the Nabataean Incense Road. *Journal of Eastern Mediterranean Archaeology and Heritage Studies*, **1** (1), 24–53.

Fantalkin, A. (2011). Why Did Nebuchadnezzer II Destroy Ashkelon in Kislev 604 B.C.E.? In I. Finkelstein & N. Na'aman, eds., *The Fire Signals of Lachish: Studies in the Archaeology and History of Israel in the Late Bronze Age, Iron Age, and Persian Period in Honor of David Ussishkin*. Winona Lake, IN: Eisenbrauns, pp. 87–111.

Fantalkin, A. (2015). Coarse Kitchen and Household Pottery as an Indicator for Egyptian Presence in the Southern Levant: A Diachronic Perspective. In M. Spataro & A. Villing, eds., *Ceramics, Cuisine and Culture: The Archaeology and Science of Kitchen Pottery in the Ancient Mediterranean World*. Oxford: Oxbow Books, pp. 233–41.

Faust, A. (2008). Settlement and Demography in Seventh-Century Judah and the Extent and Intensity of Sennacherib's Campaign. *Palestine Exploration Quarterly*, **140**(3), 168–94.

Faust, A. (2012). *Judah in the Neo-Babylonian Period: The Archaeology of Desolation*, Atlanta, GA: Society of Biblical Literature.

Faust, A. (2018). The Assyrian Century in the Southern Levant: An Overview of the Reality on the Ground. In S. Aster & A. Faust, eds., *The Southern Levant under Assyrian Domination*. University Park, PA: Eisenbrauns, pp. 20–55.

Faust, A. (2021). *The Neo-Assyrian Empire in the Southwest: Imperial Domination & its Consequences*, Oxford: Oxford University Press.

Fedele, F. (2014). Camels, Donkeys and Caravan Trade: An Emerging Context from Baraqish, Ancient Yathill (Wadi al-Jawf, Yemen). *Anthropozoologica*, **49**(2), 177–94.

Fedele, F. (2017). New Data on Domestic and Wild Camels (Camelus drome-darius and Camelus sp.) in Sabaean and Minaean Yemen. In M. Mashkour & M. Beech, eds., *Archaeozoology of the Near East 9*. Oxford: Oxbow, pp. 286–311.

Fessler, H. (2016). *Transit Corridors and Assyrian Strategy: Case Studies from the 8th–7th Century BCE Southern Levant* (Unpublished Ph.D. Dissertation), University of California, Los Angeles.

Finkelstein, I. (1992). Ḥorvat Qiṭmīt and the Southern Trade in the Late Iron Age II. *Zeitschrift Des Deutschen Palästina-Vereins*, **108**(2), 156–70.

Finkelstein, I. (1995). *Living on the Fringe: The Archaeology and History of the Negev, Sinai and Neighbouring Regions in the Bronze and Iron Ages*, Sheffield: Sheffield Academic Press.

Finkelstein, I., Adams, M., Dunseth, Z., & Shahack-Gross, R. (2018). The Archaeology and History of the Negev and Neighbouring Areas in the Third Millennium BCE: A New Paradigm. *Tel Aviv*, **45**(1), 63–88.

Finkelstein, I., Gadot, Y., & Langgut, D. (2022). The Unique Specialised Economy of Judah under Assyrian Rule and its Impact on the Material Culture of the Kingdom. *Palestine Exploration Quarterly*, **154**(4), 261–79.

Finkelstein, I., & Römer, T. (2014). Comments on the Historical Background of the Jacob Narrative in Genesis. *Zeitschrift für die alttestamentliche Wissenschaft*, **126**(3), 317–38.

Fleming, D. (2012). *The Legacy of Israel in Judah's Bible: History, Politics, and the Reinscribing of Tradition*, Cambridge: Cambridge University Press.

Fleming, D. (2021). *Yahweh before Israel: Glimpses of History in a Divine Name*, Cambridge: Cambridge University Press.

Fox, R., & Harrell, K. (2008). An Invitation to War: Constructing Alliances and Allegiances through Mycenean Palatial Feasts. In S. Baker, M. Allen, S. Middle, & K. Poole, eds., *Food and Drink in Archaeology I: University of Nottingham Postgraduate Conference 2007*. Totnes: Prospect Books, pp. 20–7.

Franklin, M. (2015). Diaspora Foodways. In K. Metheny & M. Beaudry, eds., *Archaeology of Food: An Encyclopedia*. New York: Rowman & Littlefield, pp. 133–35.

Freud, L. (1999). Pottery: Iron Age. In I. Beit-Arieh, ed., *Tel 'Ira: A Stronghold in the Biblical Negev*. Tel Aviv: Institute of Archaeology, Tel Aviv University, pp. 189–289.

Freud, L. (2007). Iron Age Pottery. In I. Beit-Arieh, ed., *Horvat 'Uza and Horvat Radum: Two Fortresses in the Biblical Negev*. Tel Aviv: Institute of Archaeology, Tel Aviv University, pp. 77–121.

Freud, L. (2014). Local Production of Edomite Cooking Pots in the Beersheba Valley: Petrographic Analyses from Tel Malhata, Horvat 'Uza and Horvat Qitmit. In J. M. Tebes, ed., *Unearthing the Wilderness: Studies on the History and Archaeology of the Negev and Edom in the Iron Age*. Leuven: Peeters, pp. 283–306.

Freud, L. (2015). The Pottery of Strata V–III. In I. Beit-Arieh & L. Freud, eds., *Tel Malhata: A Central City in the Biblical Negev*. Winona Lake, IN: Eisenbrauns, pp. 153–236.

Freud, L., & Reshef, N. (2015). Small Finds from the Iron Age. In I. Beit-Arieh & L. Freud, eds., *Tel Malhata: A Central City in the Biblical Negev*. Winona Lake, IN: Eisenbrauns, pp. 627–67.

Garfinkel, Y., & Mendel-Geberovich, A. (2020). Hierarchy, Geography and Epigraphy: Administration in the Kingdom of Judah. *Oxford Journal of Archaeology*, **39**(2), 159–76.

Garr, W. R. (1985). *Dialect Geography of Syria-Palestine, 1000–586 B.C.E*, Philadelphia: University of Pennsylvania.

Germany, S. (2022). The "Edom Texts" in Samuel-Kings in Inner- and Extrabiblical Perspective. In B. Hensel, E. Ben Zvi, and D. Edelman, eds., *About Edom and Idumea in the Persian Period: Recent Research and Approaches from Archaeology, Hebrew Bible Studies and Ancient Near Eastern Studies*. Sheffield: Equinox, pp. 363–91.

Gero, J., & Conkey, M., eds. (1991). *Engendering Archaeology: Women and Prehistory*, Cambridge, MA: Basil Blackwell.

Glueck, N. (1967). Some Edomite Pottery from Tell el-Kheleifeh. *Bulletin of the American Schools of Oriental Research*, **188**, 8–38.

Goldsmith, D., Ben-Dov, R., & Kertesz, T. (1999). Miscellaneous Finds. In I. Beit-Arieh, ed., *Tel 'Ira: A Stronghold in the Biblical Negev*. Tel Aviv: Institute of Archaeology, Tel Aviv University, pp. 444–75.

Golub, M. (2014). The Distribution of Personal Names in the Land of Israel and Transjordan during the Iron II Period. *Journal of the American Oriental Society*, **134**(4), 621–42.

Golub, M. (2017). Personal Names in Judah in the Iron Age II. *Journal of Semitic Studies*, **62**(1), 19–58.

Gosselain, O. (1998). Social and Technical Identity in a Clay Crystal Ball. In M. Stark, ed., *The Archaeology of Social Boundaries, Smithsonian Series in Archaeological Inquiry*. Washington D.C.: Smithsonian Institution Press, pp. 78–106.

Gropp, D. M. (2001). *Wadi Daliyeh II: The Samaria Papyri from Wadi Daliyeh*, Oxford: Clarendon Press.

Guillaume, P. (2013). The Myth of the Edomite Threat. In R. Lehmann & A. Zernecke, eds., *Schrift und Sprache*. Mainz: Hartmut Spenner, pp. 97–108.

Gunneweg, J., & Balla, M. (2002). Appendix 1: Instrumental Neutron Activation Analysis, Busayra and Judah. In P. Bienkowski, ed., *Busayra: Excavations by Crystal-M. Bennett 1971–1980*. Oxford: Oxford University Press, pp. 483–5.

Gunneweg, J., Beier, T., Diehl, U., Lambrecht, D., & Mommsen, H. (1991). "Edomite," "Negebite," and "Midianite" Pottery from the Negev Desert and Jordan: Instrumental Neutron Activation Analysis Results. *Archaeometry*, **33**(2), 239–53.

Gunneweg, J., & Mommsen, H. (1990). Instrumental Neutron Activation Analysis and the Origin of Some Cult Objects and Edomite Vessels from the Horvat Qitmit Shrine. *Archaeometry*, **32**(1), 7–18.

Gunneweg, J., & Mommsen, H. (1995). Instrumental Neutron Activation Analysis of Vessels and Cult Objects. In I. Beit-Arieh, ed., *Horvat Qitmit: An Edomite Shrine in the Biblical Negev*. Tel Aviv: Institute of Archaeology, Tel Aviv University, pp. 280–6.

Haiman, M., & Goren, Y. (1992). 'Negbite' Pottery: New Aspects and Interpretations and the Role of Pastoralism in Designating Ceramic Technology. In O. Bar-Yosef & A. Khazanov, eds., *Pastoralism in the Levant: Archaeological Materials in Anthropological Perspectives*. Madison, WI: Prehistory, pp. 143–51.

Hakker-Orion, D. (2007). The Faunal Remains. In R. Cohen & H. Bernick-Greenberg, eds., *Excavations at Kadesh Barnea (Tell el-Qudeirat) 1976–1982*. Jerusalem: Israel Antiquities Authority, pp. 285–302.

Halbwachs, M. (1992). *On Collective Memory*. (L. Coser, Trans.), Chicago: University of Chicago Press.

Hamori, E. (2011). Echoes of Gilgamesh in the Jacob Story. *Journal of Biblical Literature*, **130**(4), 625–42.

Hart, S. (1988). Excavations at Ghrareh, 1986: Preliminary Report. *Levant*, **20**(1), 89–99.

Hausleiter, A. (2014). Pottery Groups of the Late 2nd / Early 1st Millennia BC in Northwest Arabia and New Evidence from the Excavations at Tayma. In M. Luciani & A. Hausleiter, eds., *Recent Trends in the Study of Late Bronze Age Ceramics in Syro-Mesopotamia and Neighbouring Regions: Proceedings of the International Workshop in Berlin, 2–5 November 2006*. Rahden, DE: Verlag Marie Leidorf, pp. 399–434.

Hausleiter, A., & Schaudig, H. (2016). Rock Relief and Cuneiform Inscription of King Nabonidus at al-Ḥāʾiṭ (Province of Ḥāʾil, Saudi Arabia), Ancient Padakku. *Zeitschrift für Orient-Archäologie*, **9**, 224–240.

Hendel, R. (1987). *The Epic of the Patriarch: The Jacob Cycle and the Narrative Traditions of Canaan and Israel*, Atlanta, GA: Scholars Press.

Hendel, R. (2005). *Remembering Abraham: Culture, Memory, and History in the Hebrew Bible*, Oxford: Oxford University Press.

Hendel, R. (2010). Cultural Memory. In R. Hendel, ed., *Reading Genesis: Ten Methods*. Cambridge: Cambridge University Press, pp. 28–46.

Hensel, B. (2021a). Edom in the Jacob Cycle (Gen *25–35): New Insights on its Positive Relations with Israel, the Literary-Historical Development of its Role, and its Historical Background(s). In B. Hensel, ed., *The History of the Jacob Cycle (Genesis 25–35): Recent Research on the Compilation,* the Redaction and the Reception of the Biblical Narrative and its Historical and Cultural Contexts. Tübingen: Mohr Siebeck, pp. 57–133.

Hensel, B. (2021b). The History of the Jacob Cycle in Recent Research. In B. Hensel, ed., *The History of the Jacob Cycle (Genesis 25–35): Recent Research on the Compilation, the Redaction and the Reception of the Biblical Narrative and its Historical and Cultural Contexts.* Tübingen: Mohr Siebeck, pp. 1–9.

Hensel, B. (2021c). Tightening the Bonds between Edom and Israel (Gen 33:1–17*): On the Further Development of Edom's Role within the Fortschreibung of the Jacob Cycle in the Exilic and Early Persian Periods. *Vetus Testamentum*, **71**, 397–417.

Hensel, B., Ben Zvi, E., & Edelman, D., eds. (2022). *About Edom and Idumea in the Persian Period: Recent Research and Approaches from Archaeology, Hebrew Bible Studies and Ancient Near East Studies*, Sheffield: Equinox.

Herzog, Z. (2002). The Fortress Mound at Tel Arad: An Interim Report. *Tel Aviv*, **29**(1), 3–109.

Hogue, T. (2022). For God, King and Country: Cult and Territoriality in the Iron Age Levant. *Levant*, **54**(3), 347–58.

Hunt, A. (2015). *Palace Ware Across the Neo-Assyrian Imperial Landscape: Social Value and Semiotic Meaning*, Leiden: Brill.

Intilia, A. (2013). Qurayyah Painted Ware: A Reassessment of 40 Years of Research on its Origins, Chronology and Distribution. In M. Luciani, ed., *The Archaeology of North Arabia: Oases and Landscapes. Proceedings of the International Congress held at the University of Vienna, 5–8 December, 2013.* Vienna: Verlag der Österreichen Akademie der Wissenschaften, pp. 175–256.

Iserlis, M., & Thareani, Y. (2011). Petrographic Analysis. In Y. Thareani, ed., *Tel 'Aroer: The Iron Age II Caravan Town and the Hellenistic Settlement.* Jerusalem: Nelson Glueck School of Biblical Archaeology, pp. 179–87.

Israel, Survey. (1985). *Atlas of Israel: Cartography, Physical and Human Geography*, Tel Aviv: Macmillan.

Itkin, E. (2020). Horvat Tov: A Late Iron Age Fortress in the Northeastern Negev. *Tel Aviv*, **47**, 65–88.

Jaffe, A., Androutsopoulos, J., Sebba, M., & Johnson, S., eds. (2012). *Orthography as Social Action: Scripts, Spelling, Identity and Power*, Berlin: De Gruyter.

Jiménez, G. A., Montón-Subías, S., & Romero, M. S., eds. (2011). *Guess Who's Coming to Dinner: Feasting Rituals in the Prehistoric Societies of Europe and the Near East*, Oxford: Oxbow Books.

Jones, S. (1997). *The Archaeology of Ethnicity: Constructing Identities in the Past and Present*, New York: Routledge.

Kagan, E., Langgut, D., Boaretto, E., Neumann, F., & Stein, M. (2015). Dead Sea Levels During the Bronze and Iron Ages. *Radiocarbon*, **57**(2), 237–52.

Keane, W. (2003). Semiotics and the Social Analysis of Material Things. *Language & Communication*, **23**, 409–25.

Kelley, J. (2009). Toward a New Synthesis of the God of Edom and Yahweh. *Antiguo Oriente*, **7**, 255–80.

King, P., & Stager, L. (2001). *Life in Biblical Israel*, Louisville, KY: Westminster John Knox Press.

Klassen, S., & Danielson, A. (2023). Copper Trade Networks from the Arabah: Re-assessing the Impact on Early Iron Age Moab. In E. Ben-Yosef & I. Jones, eds., *"And in Length of Days Understanding" (Job 12:12): Essays on Archaeology in the Eastern Mediterranean and Beyond in Honor of Thomas E. Levy*. Berlin: Springer Nature, pp. 1201–26.

Kletter, R. (1996). *The Judean Pillar-Figurines and the Archaeology of Asherah*, Oxford: Tempus Reparatum.

Kletter, R. (1999). Human and Animal Clay Figurines. In I. Beit-Arieh, ed., *Tel 'Ira: A Stronghold in the Biblical Negev*. Tel Aviv: Institute of Archaeology, Tel Aviv University, pp. 374–85.

Kletter, R. (2015). Iron Age Figurines. In I. Beit-Arieh & L. Freud, eds., *Tel Malhata: A Central City in the Biblical Negev*. Winona Lake, IN: Eisenbrauns, pp. 545–73.

Knauf, E. (1988). *Midian: Untersuchungen zur Geschichte Palästinas und Nordarabiens am Ende des 2. Jahrtausends v. Chr.*, Wiesbaden: Harrassowitz.

Knauf, E. (1992a). Seir. In D. N. Freedman, ed., *Anchor Yale Bible Dictionary Vol. 5*. New York: Doubleday, pp. 1072–3.

Knauf, E. (1992b). Teman. In D. N. Freedman, ed., *Anchor Bible Dictionary Vol. 6*. New York: Doubleday, pp. 347–8.

Knauf, E. (1999). Qos. In K. van der Toorn, B. Becking, & P. van der Horst, eds., *Dictionary of Deities and Demons in the Bible*. Leiden: Brill, pp. 674–7.

Koch, I. (2018). Introductory Framework for Assyrian-Levantine Colonial Encounters. *Semitica*, **60**, 367–96.

Koch, I. (2022). Israel and Assyria, Judah and Assyria. In K. Keimer & G. Pierce, eds., *The Ancient Israelite World*. New York: Routledge, pp. 693–712.

Koch, I., & Sapir-Hen, L. (2018). Beersheba-Arad Valley during the Assyrian Period. *Semitica*, **60**, 427–52.

Koehler, L. and Baumgartner, W. (2001). *The Hebrew and Aramaic Lexicon of the Old Testament*. Leiden: Brill.

Krause, J. (2008). Tradition, History, and Our Story: Some Observations on Jacob and Esau in the Books of Obadiah and Malachi. *Journal for the Study of the Old Testament*, **32**(4), 475–86.

Kurtz, D. (2001). *Political Anthropology: Paradigms and Power*, Boulder, CO: Westview Press.

Langgut, D., Finkelstein, I., Litt, T., Neumann, F., & Stern, M. (2015). Vegetation and Climate Changes During the Bronze and Iron Ages (~3600–600 BCE) in the Southern Levant Based on Palynological Records. *Radiocarbon*, **57**(2), 217–35.

Langgut, D., Neumann, F. H., Stein, M. et al. (2014). Dead Sea Pollen Record and History of Human Activity in the Judean Highlands (Israel) from the Intermediate Bronze into the Iron Ages (~2500–500 BCE). *Palynology*, **38** (2), 280–302.

Lemaire, A. (1988). Hadad l'Édomite ou Hadad l'Araméen? *Biblische Notizen*, **43**, 14–18.

Lemaire, A. (2011). The Evolution of the 8th-Century B.C.E. Jerusalem Temple. In I. Finkelstein and N. Na'aman, eds., *The Fire Signals of Lachish: Studies in the Archaeology and History of Israel in the Late Bronze Age, Iron Age, and Persian Period in Honor of David Ussishkin*. Winona Lake, IN: Eisenbrauns, pp. 195–202.

Levy, T., Najjar, M., & Ben-Yosef, E., eds. (2014). *New Insights into the Iron Age Archaeology of Edom, Southern Jordan*, Los Angeles: Cotsen Institute of Archaeology.

Lewis, T. (2020). *The Origin and Character of God: Ancient Israelite Religion through the Lens of Divinity*, New York: Oxford University Press.

Lindner, M., & Knauf, E. (1997). Between the Plateau and the Rocks Edomite Economic and Social Structure. In *Studies in the History and Archaeology of Jordan*, **6**, 261–4.

Lindsay, J. (1976). The Babylonian Kings and Edom. *Palestine Exploration Quarterly*, **108**, 23–39.

Lipschits, O. (2005). *The Fall and Rise of Jerusalem: Judah under Babylonian Rule*, Winona Lake, IN: Eisenbrauns.

Luciani, M., & Alsaud, A. (2018). The New Archaeological Joint Project on the Site of Qurayyah, North-West Arabia: Results of the First Two Excavation Seasons. *Proceedings of the Seminar for Arabian Studies*, **48**, 165–183.

Lucy, S. (2005). Ethnic and Cultural Identities. In M. Diaz-Andreu, S. Lucy, S. Babić, & D. Edwards, eds., *The Archaeology of Identity: Approaches to*

Gender, Age, Status, Ethnicity and Religion. New York: Routledge, pp. 86–109.

Macdonald, M. (1997). Trade Routes and Trade Goods at the Northern End of the "Incense Road" in the First Millennium B.C. In A. Avanzini, ed., *Profumi D'Arabia: Atti del Convego.* Rome: L'Erma di Bretschneider, pp. 333–49.

Macdonald, N. (2008). *What did the Ancient Israelites Eat: Diet in Biblical Times,* Grand Rapids, MI: Eerdmans.

Magee, P. (2015). When was the Dromedary Domesticated in the Ancient Near East? In M. van Ess and R. Eichmann, eds., *Sonderdruk aus Zeitschrift für Orient-Archäologie Band 8.* Berlin: Ernst Wasmuth Verlag, pp. 252–77.

Magness, J. (2014). Conspicuous Consumption: Dining on Meat in the Ancient Mediterranean World and Near East. In P. Altmann & J. Fu, eds., *Feasting in the Archaeology and Texts of the Bible and the Ancient Near East.* Winona Lake, IN: Eisenbrauns, pp. 33–60.

Martin, M., & Finkelstein, I. (2013). Iron IIA Pottery from the Negev Highlands: Petrographic Investigation and Historical Implications. *Tel Aviv,* **40**(1), 6–45.

Mazar, E. (1985). Edomite Pottery at the End of the Iron Age. *Israel Exploration Journal,* **35**(4), 253–69.

McCarter, P. K. (1987). Aspects of the Religion of the Israelite Monarchy: Biblical and Epigraphic Data. In P. Miller, P. Hanson, & S. D. McBride, eds., *Ancient Israelite Religion: Essays in Honor of F. M. Cross.* Philadelphia, PA: Fortress Press, pp. 137–55.

Meyers, C. (1988). *Discovering Eve: Ancient Israelite Women in Context,* New York: Oxford University Press.

Meyers, C. (2007). From Field Crops to Food: Attributing Gender and Meaning to Bread Production in Iron Age Israel. In D. Edwards & C. McCullough, eds., *The Archaeology of Difference: Gender, Ethnicity, Class and the 'Other' in Antiquity.* Boston, MA: American Schools of Oriental Research, pp. 67–84.

Meyers, C. (2012). The Function of Feasts: An Anthropological Perspective on Israelite Religious Festivals. In S. Olyan, ed., *Social Theory and the Study of Israelite Religion: Essays in Retrospect and Prospect.* Atlanta: Society of Biblical Literature, pp. 141–68.

Miller, R. (2021). *Yahweh: Origin of a Desert God,* Göttingen: Vandenhoeck & Ruprecht.

Mills, B. (2007). Performing the Feast: Visual Display and Suprahousehold Commensalism in the Puebloan Southwest. *American Antiquity,* **72**(2), 210–39.

Motro, H. (2011). Archaeozoological Analysis of the Faunal Remains. In Y. Thareani, ed., *Tel ʿAroer: The Iron Age II Caravan Town and the Hellenistic Settlement*. Jerusalem: Nelson Glueck School of Biblical Archaeology, pp. 265–97.

Multhoff, A. (2019). Merchant and Marauder—The Adventures of a Sabaean Clansman. *Arabian Archaeology and Epigraphy*, **30**, 239–62.

Na'aman, N. (2003). Ostracon No. 40 from Arad Reconsidered. In C. den Hertog, U. Hübner, & S. Münger, eds., *Saxa Loquentur: Studien zur Archäologie Palästinas/Israels Festschrift für Volkmar Fritz zum 65. Geburtstag*. Münster: Ugarit-Verlag, pp. 199–204.

Nakhai, B. A. (2014). The Household as Sacred Space. In R. Albertz, B. A. Nakhai, S. Olyan, & R. Schmitt, eds., *Family and Household Religion: Toward a Synthesis of Old Testament Studies, Archaeology, Epigraphy, and Cultural Studies*. Winona Lake, IN: Eisenbrauns, pp. 53–72.

Nash, D. (2018). Edom, Judah, and Converse Constructions of Israeliteness in Genesis 36. *Vetus Testamentum*, **68**, 111–28.

Nelson, K. (2015). Cooking Vessels, Ceramic. In K. Metheny & M. Beaudry, eds., *Archaeology of Food: An Encyclopedia*. New York: Rowman & Littlefield, pp. 116–8.

Nielsen, H. F. (2005). *From Dialect to Standard: English in England 1154–1776*, Odense: University Press of Southern Denmark.

Nyström, S. (2016). Names and Meaning. In C. Hough, ed., *The Oxford Handbook of Names and Naming*. Oxford: Oxford University Press, pp. 39–51.

van Oorschot, J. & Witte, M., eds. (2017). *The Origins of Yahwism*. Berlin: De Gruyter.

Osborne, J. (2013). Sovereignty and Territoriality in the City-State: A Case Study from the Amuq Valley, Turkey. *Journal of Anthropological Archaeology*, **32**(4), 774–90.

Osborne, J. (2020). *The Syro-Anatolian City-States: An Iron Age Culture*, Oxford: Oxford University Press.

Pace, L. (2014). Feasting and Everyday Meals in the World of the Hebrew Bible: The Relationship Reexamined through Material Culture and Texts. In P. Altmann & J. Fu, eds., *Feasting in the Archaeology and Texts of the Bible and the Ancient Near East*. Winona Lake, IN: Eisenbrauns, pp. 179–98.

Peters, K. (2016). *Hebrew Lexical Semantics and Daily Life in Ancient Israel: What's Cooking in Biblical Hebrew?*, Leiden: Brill.

Pollock, S. ed. (2012). *Between Feasts and Daily Meals: Towards an Archaeology of Commensal Spaces*, Berlin: Edition Topoi.

Porter, B. (2004). Authority, Polity and Tenuous Elites in Iron Age Edom (Jordan). *Oxford Journal of Archaeology*, **23**(4), 373–95.

Porter, B. (2011). Feeding the Community: Objects, Scarcity and Commensality in the Early Iron Age Southern Levant. *Journal of Mediterranean Archaeology*, **24**(1), 27–54.

Porter, B. (2022). The Invention of Ancient Moab. In K. Keimer & G. Pierce, eds., *The Ancient Israelite World*. New York: Routledge, pp. 619–38.

Reich, R. (1992). Palaces and Residences in the Iron Age. In A. Kempinski & R. Reich, eds., *The Architecture of Ancient Israel: From the Prehistoric to the Persian Periods*. Jerusalem: Israel Exploration Society, pp. 202–22.

Retsö, J. (2003). *The Arabs in Antiquity: Their History from the Assyrians to the Umayyads*, London: Routledge.

Rice, P. (1987). *Pottery Analysis: A Sourcebook*, Chicago, IL: University of Chicago Press.

Rollston, C. (2014). The Iron Age Edomite Script and Language: Methodological Strictures and Preliminary Statements. In T. Levy, M. Najjar, & E. Ben-Yosef, eds., *New Insights into the Iron Age Archaeology of Edom, Southern Jordan*. Los Angeles: Cotsen Institute of Archaeology, pp. 961–76.

Routledge, B. (2003). The Antiquity of the Nation? Critical Reflections from the Ancient Near East. *Nations and Nationalism*, **9**(2), 213–33.

Routledge, B. (2004). *Moab in the Iron Age: Hegemony, Polity, Archaeology*, Philadelphia, PA: University of Pennsylvania Press.

Sanders, S. (2015). When the Personal Became Political: An Onomastic Perspective on the Rise of Yahwism. *Hebrew Bible and Ancient Israel*, **4**, 78–105.

Sapir-Hen, L., & Ben-Yosef, E. (2013). The Introduction of Domestic Camels to the Southern Levant: Evidence from the Aravah Valley. *Tel Aviv*, **40**, 277–85.

Schipper, B. (2010). Egypt and the Kingdom of Judah under Josiah and Jehoiakim. *Tel Aviv*, **37**(2), 200–26.

Schmid, K. (2021). Shifting Political Theologies in the Literary Development of the Jacob Cycle. In B. Hensel, ed., *The History of the Jacob Cycle (Genesis 25–35): Recent Research on the Compilation, the Redaction and the Reception of the Biblical Narrative and its Historical and Cultural Contexts*. Tübingen: Mohr Siebeck, pp. 11–34.

Schmitt, R. (2014). A Typology of Iron Age Cult Places. In R. Albertz, B. A. Nakhai, S. Olyan, & R. Schmitt, eds., *Family and Household Religion: Toward a Synthesis of Old Testament Studies, Archaeology, Epigraphy, and Cultural Studies*, Winona Lake, IN: Eisenbrauns, pp. 265–86.

Schniedewind, W. (2013). *A Social History of Hebrew: Its Origins through the Rabbinic Period*, New Haven, CT: Yale University Press.

Schniedewind, W. (2019). *The Finger of the Scribe: How Scribes Learned to Write the Bible*, Oxford: Oxford University Press.

Sebba, M., Mahootian, S., & Jonsson, C., eds. (2012). *Language Mixing and Code-Switching in Writing: Approaches to Mixed-Language Written Discourse*, New York: Routledge.

Sedman, L. (2002). The Small Finds. In P. Bienkowski, ed., *Busayra: Excavations by Crystal-M. Bennett 1971–1980*, Oxford: Oxford University Press, pp. 353–428.

Segert, S. (1997). Phoenician and the Eastern Canaanite Languages. In R. Hetzron, ed., *The Semitic Languages*. New York: Routledge, pp. 174–86.

Sergi, O. (2019). Israelite Identity and the Formation of the Israelite Polities in the Iron I–IIA Central Canaanite Highlands. *Die Welt Des Orients*, **49**(2), 206–35.

Shafer-Elliott, C. (2013). *Food in Ancient Judah: Domestic Cooking in the Time of the Hebrew Bible*, Sheffield: Equinox.

Singer-Avitz, L. (1999). Beersheba – A Gateway Community in Southern Arabian Long-Distance Trade in the Eighth Century B.C.E. *Tel Aviv*, **26** (1), 3–75.

Singer-Avitz, L. (2002). Arad: The Iron Age Pottery Assemblages. *Tel Aviv*, **29** (1), 110–214.

Singer-Avitz, L. (2014). Edomite Pottery in Judah in the Eighth Century BCE. In J. M. Tebes, ed., *Unearthing the Wilderness: Studies on the History and Archaeology of the Negev and Edom in the Iron Age*. Leuven: Peeters, pp. 267–82.

Smith, M. (2005). Networks, Territories, and the Cartography of Ancient States. *Annals of the Association of American Geographers*, **95**(4), 832–49.

Smith, M. (2016). *Where the Gods Are: Spatial Dimensions of Anthropomorphism in the Biblical World*, New Haven, CT: Yale University Press.

Smith, N. (2009). *Social Boundaries and State Formation in Ancient Edom: A Comparative Ceramic Approach* (Unpublished Ph.D. Dissertation), University of California, San Diego.

Smith, N., Najjar, M., & Levy, T. (2014). New Perspectives on the Iron Age Edom Steppe and Highlands: Khirbat al-Malayqtah, Khirbat al-Kur, Khirbat al-Iraq Shmaliya, and Tawilan. In T. Levy, M. Najjar, & E. Ben-Yosef, eds., *New Insights into the Iron Age Archaeology of Edom, Southern Jordan*. Los Angeles: Cotsen Institute of Archaeology, pp. 247–96.

Smoak, J. (2022). Religion in the House in Ancient Israel. In K. H. Keimer & G. A. Pierce, eds., *The Ancient Israelite World*. New York: Routledge, pp. 421–33.

Sneh, A., Bartov, T., Weissbrod, T., & Rosensaft, M. (1998). Geological Map of Israel, 1:200,000. http://www.gsi.gov.il (Accessed: April 19, 2019).

Stager, L., Master, D., & Schloen, J. D. (2008). *Ashkelon 3: The Seventh Century B.C.*, Winona Lake, IN: Eisenbrauns.

Stowers, S. (2008). Theorizing the Religion of Ancient Households and Families. In J. Bodel & S. Olyan, eds., *Household and Family Religion in Antiquity*, Malden, MA: Blackwell, pp. 5–19.

Tebes, J. M. (2006a). Trade and Nomads: The Commercial Relations Between the Negev, Edom, and the Mediterranean in the Late Iron Age. *Journal of the Serbian Archaeological Society*, **22**, 45–62.

Tebes, J. M. (2006b). "You Shall Not Abhor an Edomite, for He is Your Brother": The Tradition of Esau and the Edomite Genealogies from an Anthropological Perspective. *Journal of Hebrew Scriptures*, **6**(6), 2–30.

Tebes, J. M. (2007a). Assyrians, Judaeans, Pastoral Groups, and the Trade Patterns in the Late Iron Age Negev. *History Compass*, **5**(2), 619–31.

Tebes, J. M. (2007b). Pottery Makers and Premodern Exchange in the Fringes of Egypt: An Approximation to the Distribution of Iron Age Midianite Pottery. *Buried History*, **43**, 11–26.

Tebes, J. M. (2011a). The Edomite Involvement in the Destruction of the First Temple: A Case of Stab-in-the-Back Tradition? *Journal for the Study of the Old Testament*, **36**(2), 219–55.

Tebes, J. M. (2011b). The Potter's Will: Spheres of Production, Distribution and Consumption of the Late Iron Age Southern Transjordan-Negev Pottery. *Strata: Bulletin of the Anglo-Israel Archaeological Society*, **29**, 61–101.

Tebes, J. M. (2013). Investigating the Painted Pottery Traditions of First-Millennium BC North-Western Arabia and Southern Levant: Chronological Data and Geographical Distribution. *Proceedings of the Seminar for Arabian Studies*, **43**, 317–36.

Tebes, J. M. (2015). Investigating the Painted Pottery Traditions of the First Millennium BC Northwestern Arabia and Southern Levant: Contexts of Discovery and Painted Decorative Motives. *ARAM*, **27**(2), 255–82.

Thareani, Y. (2010). The Spirit of Clay: "Edomite Pottery" and Social Awareness in the Late Iron Age. *Bulletin of the American Schools of Oriental Research*, **359**, 33–55.

Thareani, Y. (2011). *Tel 'Aroer: The Iron Age II Caravan Town and the Hellenistic-Early Roman Settlement*, Jerusalem: Nelson Glueck School of Biblical Archaeology.

Thareani, Y. (2014). "The Self-Destruction of Diversity": A Tale of the Last Days in Judah's Negev Towns. *Antiguo Oriente*, **12**, 185–224.

Thareani, Y. (2016). The Empire and the "Upper Sea": Assyrian Control Strategies along the Southern Levantine Coast. *Bulletin of the American Schools of Oriental Research*, **375**, 77–102.

Thareani, Y. (2017). Empires and Allies: A Longue Durée View from the Negev Desert Frontier. In O. Lipschits, Y. Gadot, & M. J. Adams, eds., *Rethinking Israel: Studies in the History and Archaeology of Ancient Israel in Honor of Israel Finkelstein*. Winona Lake, IN: Eisenbrauns, pp. 409–28.

Thareani-Sussely, Y. (2007). Ancient Caravanserais: An Archaeological View from ʿAroer. *Levant*, **39**(1), 123–41.

van der Toorn, K. (1999). Yahweh. In K. van der Toorn, B. Becking, & P. W. van der Horst, eds., *Dictionary of Deities and Demons in the Bible*. Leiden: Brill, pp. 910–9.

Twiss, K. (2012). The Archaeology of Food and Social Diversity. *Journal of Archaeological Research*, **20**(4), 357–95.

Twiss, K. (2019). *The Archaeology of Food: Identity, Politics, and Ideology in the Prehistoric and Historic Past*, Cambridge: Cambridge University Press.

Tyson, C. (2018). Peripheral Elite as Imperial Collaborators. In C. Tyson & V. Herrmann, eds., *Imperial Peripheries in the Neo-Assyrian Period*. Boulder, CO: University Press of Colorado, pp. 177–209.

Vaknin, Y., Shaar, R., Lipschits, O. et al. (2022). Reconstructing Biblical Military Campaigns using Geomagnetic Field Data. *Proceedings of the National Academy of Sciences*, **119**(44), e2209117119.

Vanderhooft, D. (1995). Edomite Dialect and Script: A Review of the Evidence. In D. Edelman, ed., *You Shall Not Abhor an Edomite for He Is Your Brother: Edom and Seir in History and Tradition*, Atlanta: Scholars Press, pp. 137–58.

Wapnish, P. (1981). Camel Caravans and Camel Pastoralists at Tell Jemmeh. *Journal of Ancient Near Eastern Studies*, **13**, 101–21.

Weis, L. (1995). Identity Formation and the Processes of "Othering": Unraveling Sexual Threads. *Educational Foundations*, **9**(1), 17–33.

Weldon, T. (2018). Sounding Black: Labeling and Perceptions of African American Voices on Southern College Campuses. In J. Reaser, E. Wilbanks, K. Wojcik, & W. Wolfram, eds., *Language Variety in the New South: Contemporary Perspectives on Change and Variation*. Chapel Hill, NC: The University of North Carolina Press, pp. 175–202.

Westbrook, R. (2005). Patronage in Ancient Near East. *Journal of the Economic and Social History of the Orient*, **48**(2), 210–33.

Whiting, C. (2007). *Complexity and Diversity in the late Iron Age Southern Levant: The Investigations of "Edomite" Archaeology and Scholarly Discourse*. Oxford: Archaeopress.

Wimmer, A., & Schiller, N. G. (2002). Methodological Nationalism and Beyond: Nation–State Building, Migration and the Social Sciences. *Global Networks*, **2**(4), 301–34.

Winnicki, J. (2009). *Late Egypt and Her Neighbours: Foreign Population in Egypt in the First Millennium BC*, Warsaw: Warsaw University.

Wöhrle, J. (2021). Jacob from Israel and Jacob from Judah: Reflections on the Formation and the Historical Backgrounds of the Jacob Story. In B. Hensel, ed., *The History of the Jacob Cycle (Genesis 25–35): Recent Research on the Compilation, the Redaction and the Reception of the Biblical Narrative and its Historical and Cultural Contexts*. Tübingen: Mohr Siebeck, pp. 135–53.

Yahalom-Mack, N. (2017). Metal Production and Trade at the Turn of the First Millennium BCE: Some Answers, New Questions. In O. Lipschits, Y. Gadot, & M. Adams, eds., *Rethinking Israel: Studies in the History and Archaeology of Ancient Israel in Honor of Israel Finkelstein*. Winona Lake, IN: Eisenbrauns, pp. 451–61.

Yamada, S. (2005). Karus on the Frontiers of the Neo-Assyrian Empire. *Orient*, **40**, 56–90.

Zadok, R. (1997). Names and Naming. In E. Meyers, ed., *Oxford Encyclopedia of Archaeology in the Near East Volume 4*. Oxford: Oxford University Press, pp. 91–6.

Zevit, Z. (2001). *The Religions of Ancient Israel: A Synthesis of Parallactic Approaches*, New York: Continuum.

Zevit, Z. (2014). The Textual and Social Embeddedness of Israelite Family Religion: Who Were the Players? Where Were the Stages? In R. Albertz, B. A. Nakhai, S. Olyan, & R. Schmitt, eds., *Family and Household Religion: Toward a Synthesis of Old Testament Studies, Archaeology, Epigraphy, and Cultural Studies*. Winona Lake, IN: Eisenbrauns, pp. 287–314.

Cambridge Elements ☰

The Archaeology of Ancient Israel

Series Editors

Aaron A. Burke
University of California, Los Angeles

Aaron A. Burke is Professor of the Archaeology of Ancient Israel and the Levant, and the Kershaw Chair of the Ancient Eastern Mediterranean Studies in the Department of Near Eastern Languages and Cultures at the University of California, Los Angeles, and member of the Cotsen Institute of Archaeology. His research and teaching interests center on the social history of the Levant and Eastern Mediterranean during the Bronze and Iron Ages at the intersections of the study of archaeology, iconography, and texts, including the Hebrew Bible. He has conducted excavations in Jaffa and Tel Dan in Israel.

Jeremy D. Smoak
University of California, Los Angeles

Jeremy D. Smoak is Senior Lecturer in the Department of Near Eastern Languages and Cultures at the University of California, Los Angeles, where he teaches on Hebrew Bible, the history of ancient Israel, and Semitic languages. He is the author of *The Priestly Blessing in Inscription and Scripture: The Early History of Numbers 6:24–26* (Oxford University Press, 2016). He has also published a variety of articles in journals related to archaeology and biblical studies. He has participated in several excavations in Israel and traveled extensively throughout the eastern Mediterranean.

Editorial Advisory Board

About the Series

The archaeology of ancient Israel is among the oldest historical archaeologies in practice. Multi-disciplinary approaches that integrate improved readings of biblical texts, new recovery techniques, pioneering scientific analyses, and advances in identity studies have dramatically changed the questions asked and the findings that follow. Elements in the Archaeology of Ancient Israel embodies these developments, providing readers with the most up-to-date assessments of a wide range of related subjects.

Cambridge Elements ≡

The Archaeology of Ancient Israel

Elements in the Series